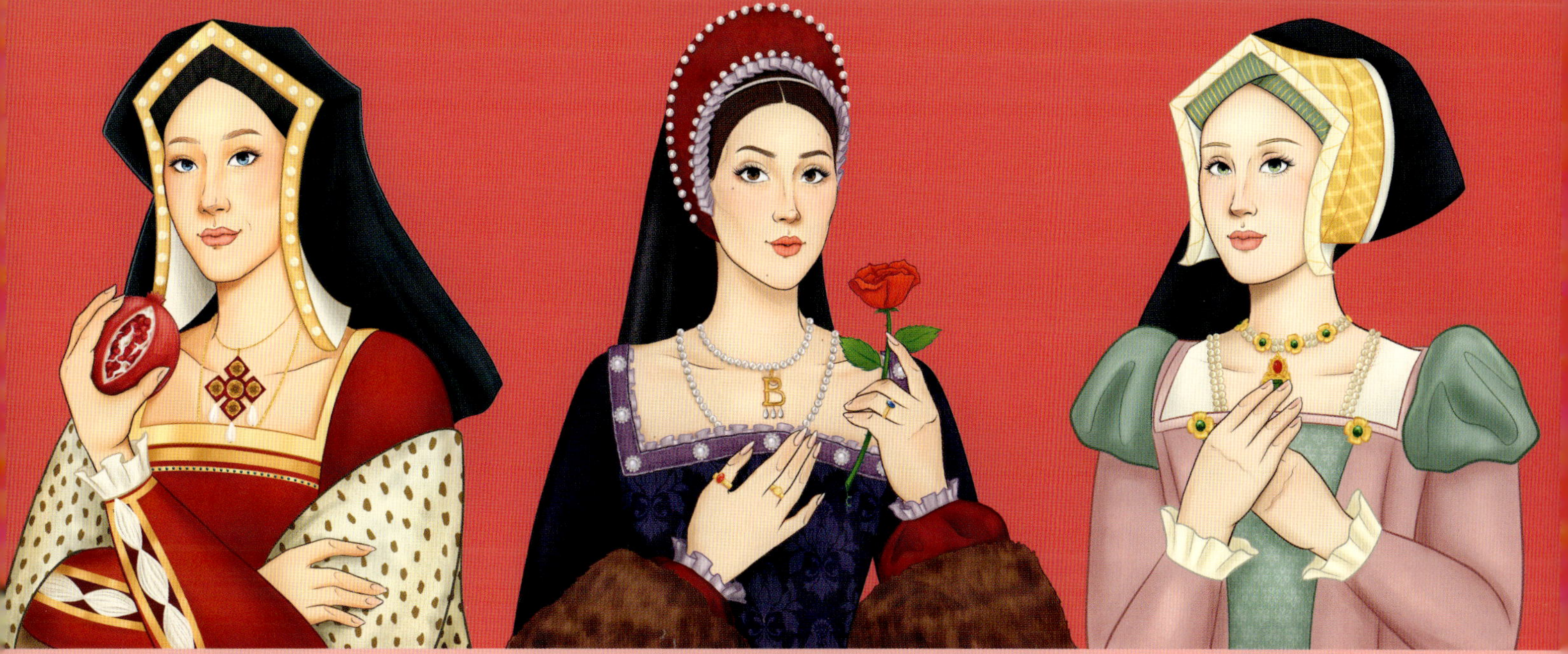

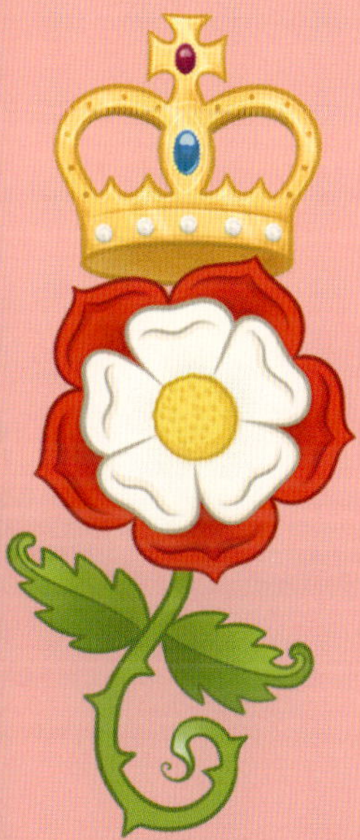

THE SIX QUEENS OF HENRY VIII

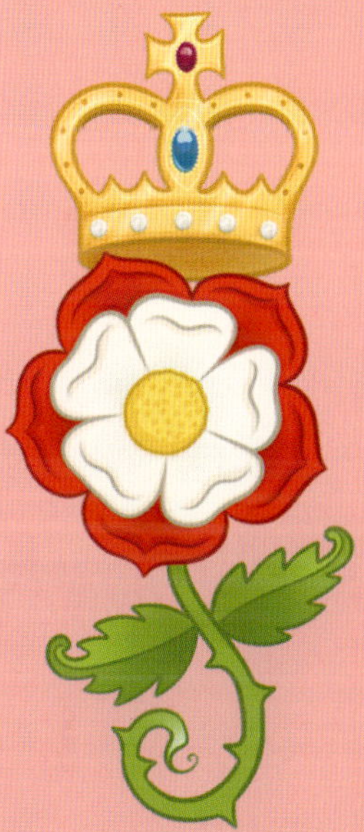

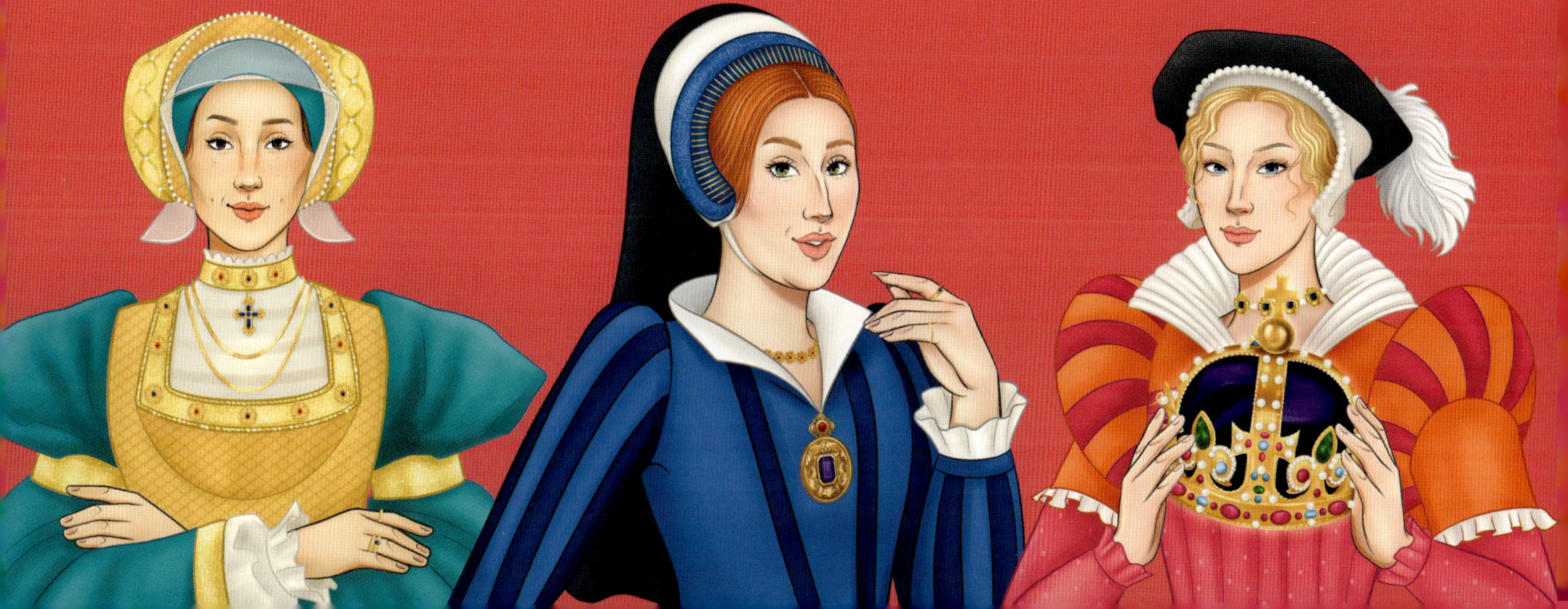

To all the women, queens or otherwise, who had to deal with Henry VIII ~ H. C-M.

To my family for your endless support, inspiration and love ~ J. A.

HODDER CHILDREN'S BOOKS
First published in Great Britain in 2024 by
Hodder and Stoughton

Text copyright © Honor Cargill-Martin, 2024
Illustrations copyright © Jaimee Andrews, 2024

Honor Cargill-Martin and Jaimee Andrews have asserted their right under the Copyright, Designs and Patents Act 1988, to be identified as the author and illustrator of this work. All rights reserved. A CIP catalogue record for this book is available from the British Library.

HB ISBN 978-1-444-97657-1
E-book ISBN 978-1-444-97658-8

3 5 7 9 10 8 6 4 2

Printed in China

MIX
Paper | Supporting responsible forestry
FSC® C104740

Hodder Children's Books
An imprint of Hachette Children's Group
Part of Hodder and Stoughton Limited
Carmelite House,
50 Victoria Embankment,
London, EC4Y 0DZ

An Hachette UK Company
www.hachette.co.uk
www.hachettechildrens.co.uk

The authorised representative in the EEA is Hachette Ireland, 8 Castlecourt Centre, Dublin 15, D15 XTP3, Ireland (email: info@hbgi.ie)

THE SIX QUEENS OF HENRY VIII

HONOR CARGILL-MARTIN

JAIMEE ANDREWS

A Word From the Author

Welcome to the **Tudor period**, one of the most turbulent and important in British history. New styles of art are flooding in from Europe and sailors are bringing back never-before-seen fruits and spices from the furthest reaches of the world. The king is popularising tennis and the new technology of book printing is spreading radical new ideas about religion. The most extraordinary place of all is the **Tudor royal court**, where every day is a whirl of ceremonies and tournaments, banquets and pageants.

Beware of being too dazzled by the splendour of the court – it's a dangerous place. All the changes happening in politics and religion have created tension, and courtiers love nothing more than plotting each other's downfalls. Things are especially risky during the reign of **Henry VIII** because although the king is educated and romantic, he's also known to be suspicious and unpredictable. At Henry's court, the most powerful positions are also the most dangerous – none more so than that of the **queen.**

You might already have heard that Henry VIII had six **(SIX!)** wives. You might even be able to tell me what happened to them (divorced, beheaded, died, divorced, beheaded, survived), but how much do you actually know about **their lives?**

It turns out that each one of Henry's six wives was an extraordinary woman in her own right. One led an army, one helped to create a whole new church and one was the first female author to publish a book under her own name in English.

Ready to meet them?

CATHERINE OF ARAGON

BIOGRAPHY

Catherine (or Catalina, as she was known in Spain) was born during a military campaign that was being led by her mother, the powerful Queen Isabella of Castille. When Catherine was just three years old, she was engaged to marry Prince Arthur, Henry VIII's older brother.

BORN: 1485, Alcala de Henares, Spain

EDUCATION: Latin, philosophy, history, theology, law

DOWRY: 200,000 crowns

ALLIES: Spain, the Holy Roman Emperor, the Pope

MARRIED HENRY VIII: 1509

DIVORCED: 1533

DIED: 1536

CHILDREN: Mary I

MOTTO: "Humble and Loyal"

Oh, Brother!

Isabella ensured her daughters were well-educated in law, history and philosophy. The only thing Catherine wasn't taught was English. When she first arrived from Spain in 1501, she and Arthur had to chat in the ancient Roman language of Latin.

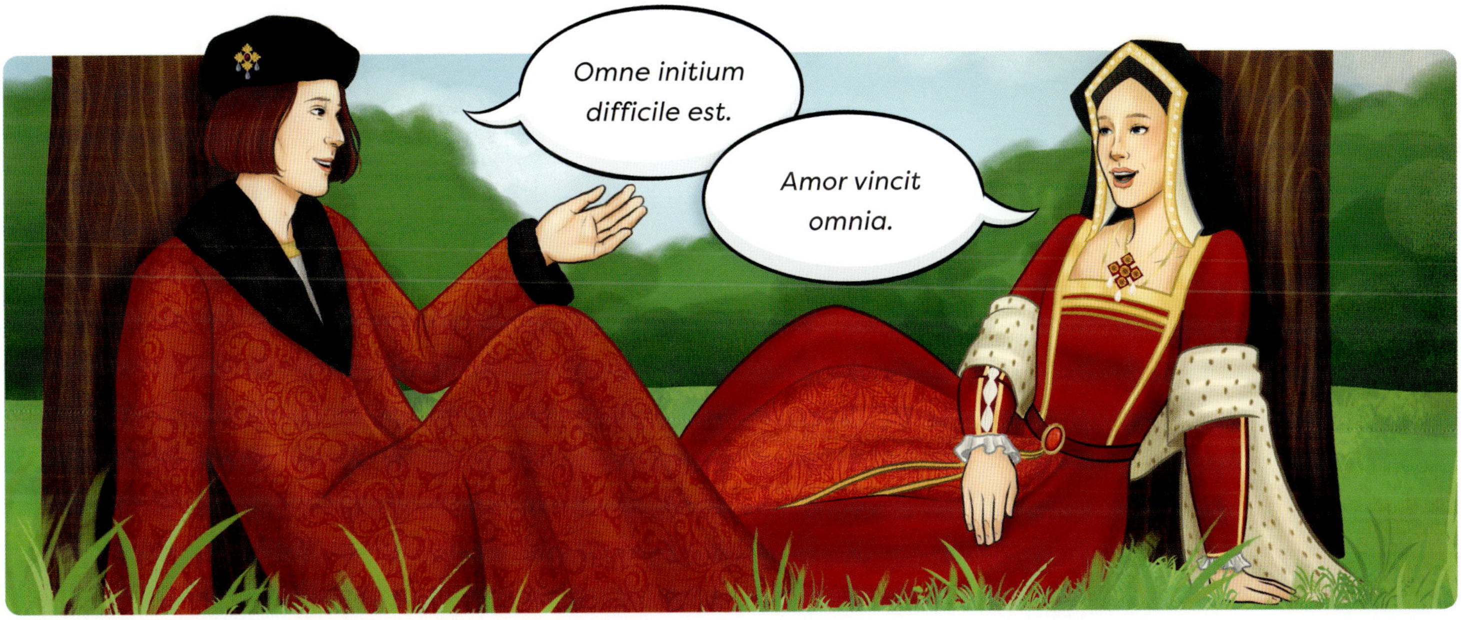
Omne initium difficile est.
Amor vincit omnia.

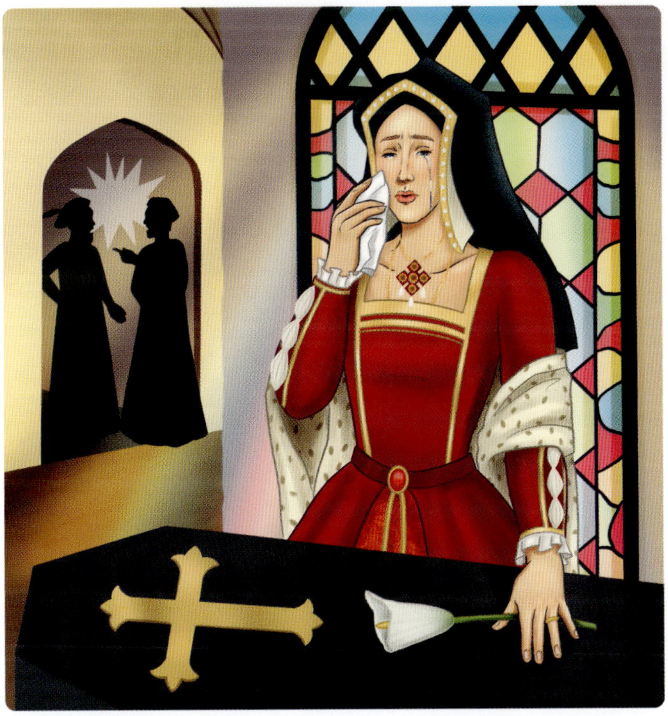

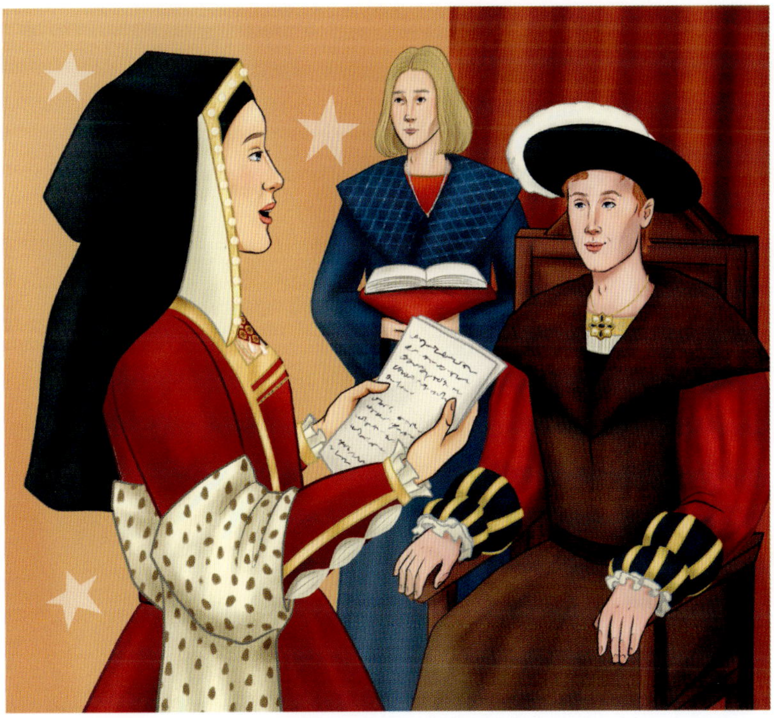

Arthur died just a few months after their wedding. This left Catherine in an awkward position, as arguments about her remarriage to his younger brother, Prince Henry, dragged on.

She learnt to play court politics and soon became Spanish ambassador to England – the first ever female ambassador in European history. Catherine began to negotiate with the King Henry VII and even learnt to use a top-secret code called cipher.

Wedding Take Two

Henry VIII wasn't always huge and smelly – when he married Catherine soon after becoming King in 1509, he was famously tall and good-looking, as well as being musical and sporty.

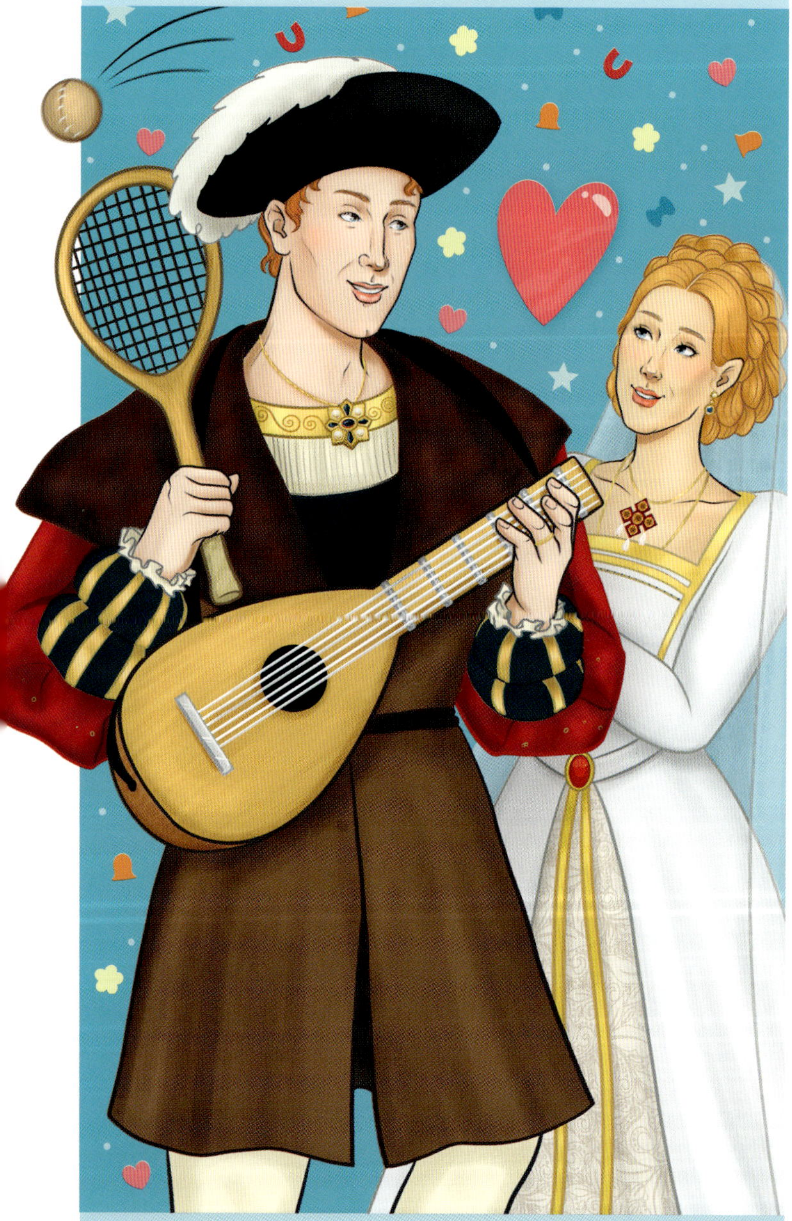

The English people were crazy for the glamorous young couple! At first everything looked rosy, but it wouldn't last forever . . .

An Heir-y Question

Medicine was less advanced in this period and babies often died very young. Catherine fell pregnant at least six times, but only one of her children survived infancy. To Henry's dismay, it was a *girl*!

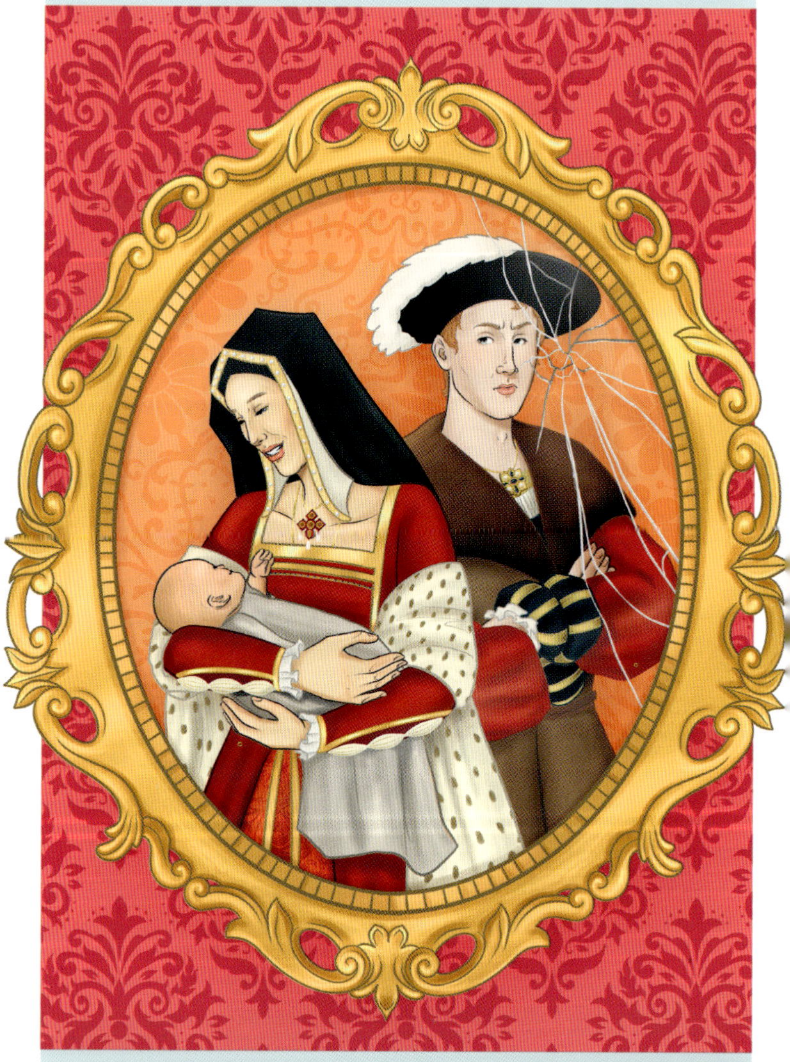

Although women could be rulers in Catherine's native Spain, the English were less open to the idea. Henry VIII became increasingly desperate to have a son to be heir to his throne, but Catherine did not provide one.

Courtroom Drama

Henry wanted out of his marriage to Catherine. Suddenly claiming it was wrong that she'd been married to his brother first, Henry asked the Pope to grant him an annulment – a type of divorce that says a marriage never really happened.

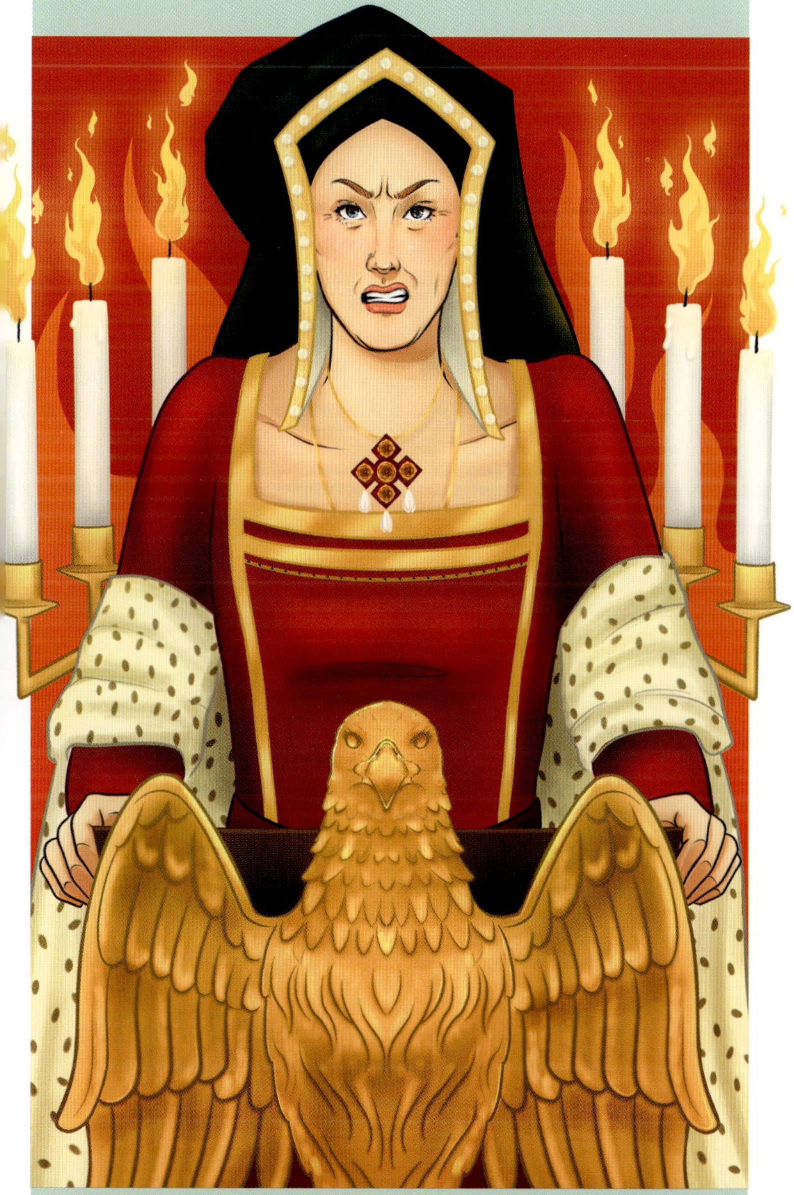

Catherine gave a powerful speech before the Pope's representatives demanding that Henry 'let her have justice and right'.

The Pope refused, so in 1533 Henry had the marriage annulled himself. He broke with Rome and established the Church of England, which he (surprise, surprise) was head of. Catherine remained as popular as ever and the French ambassador wrote that she'd win out over Henry if women had a fair say.

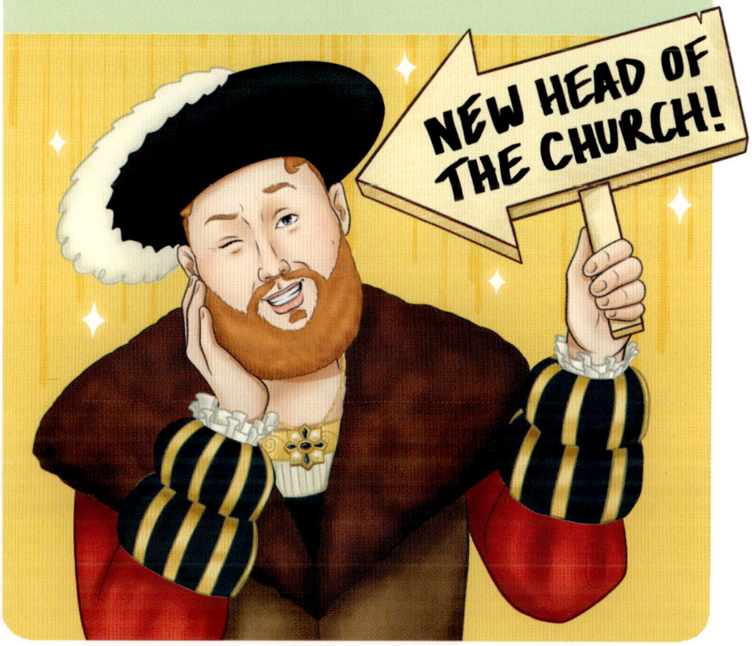
NEW HEAD OF THE CHURCH!

Catherine was sent to a series of dreary castles until she died aged just fifty. Until the end of her life, she signed her letters 'Catherine the Queen'.

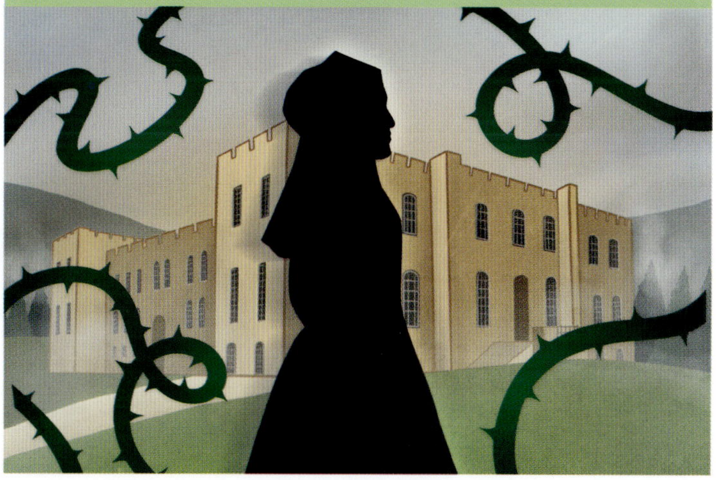

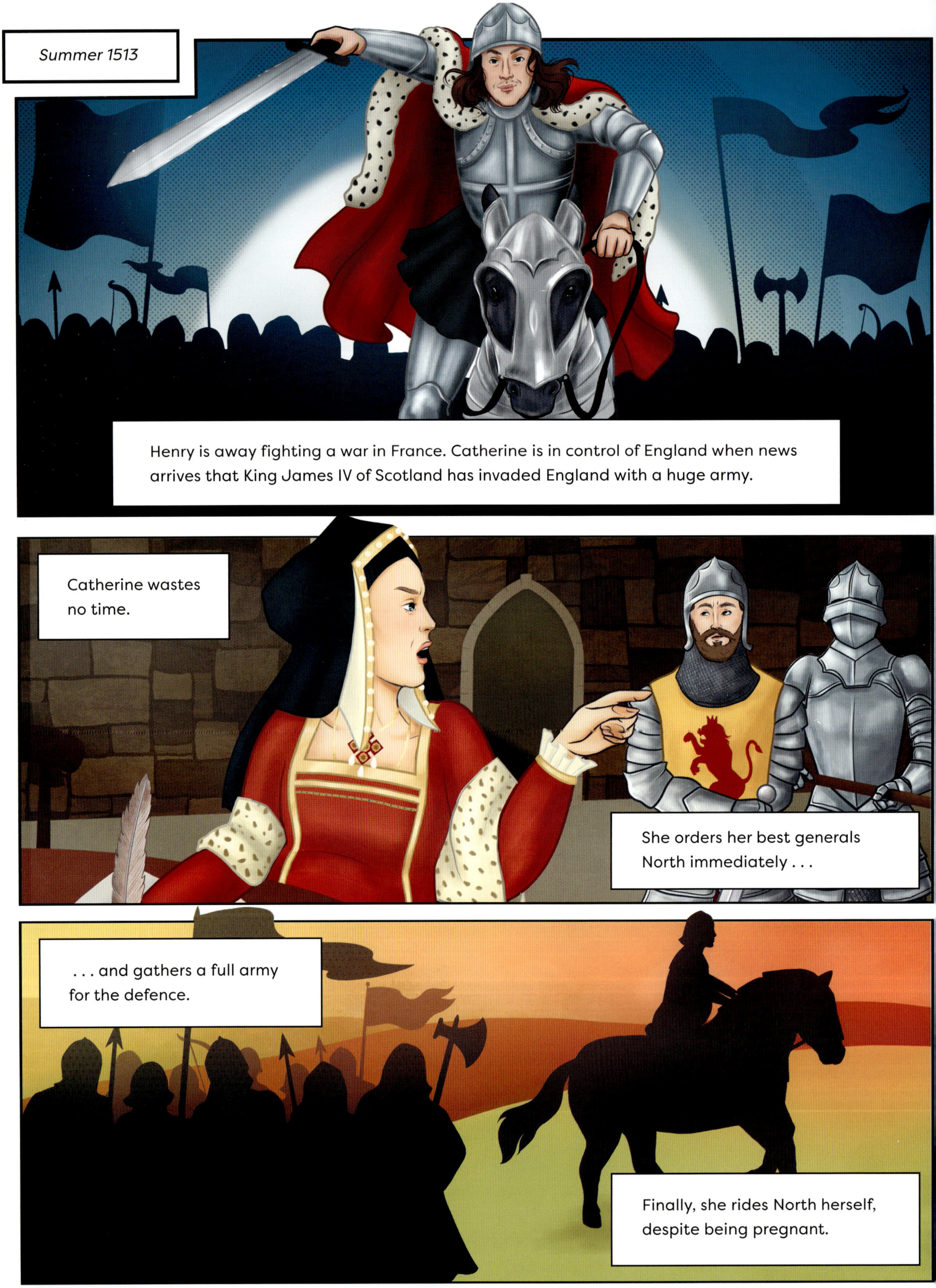
Summer 1513
Henry is away fighting a war in France. Catherine is in control of England when news arrives that King James IV of Scotland has invaded England with a huge army.
Catherine wastes no time.
She orders her best generals North immediately . . .
. . . and gathers a full army for the defence.
Finally, she rides North herself, despite being pregnant.

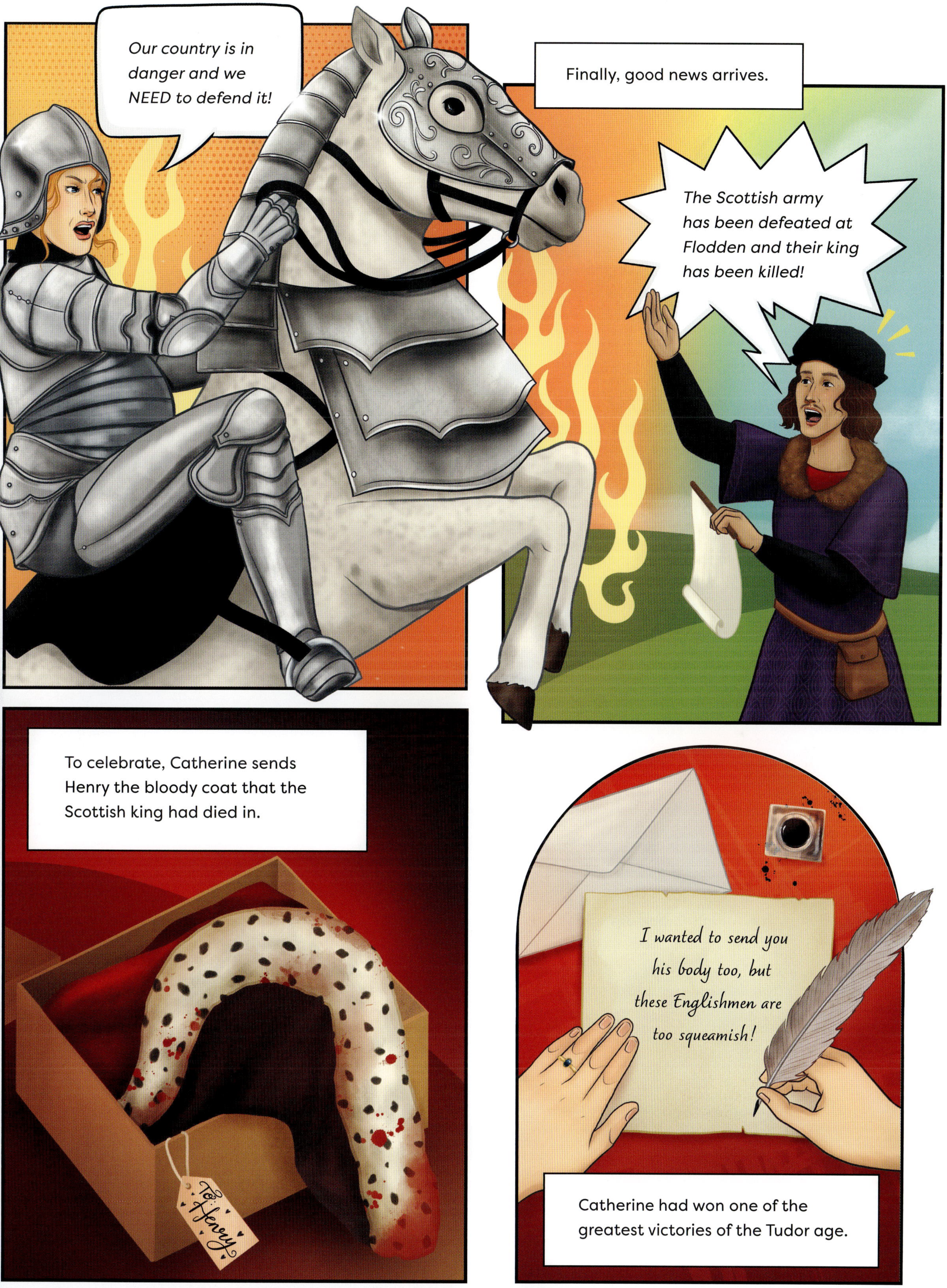
Our country is in danger and we NEED to defend it!
Finally, good news arrives.
The Scottish army has been defeated at Flodden and their king has been killed!
To celebrate, Catherine sends Henry the bloody coat that the Scottish king had died in.
To: Henry
I wanted to send you his body too, but these Englishmen are too squeamish!
Catherine had won one of the greatest victories of the Tudor age.

ANNE BOLEYN

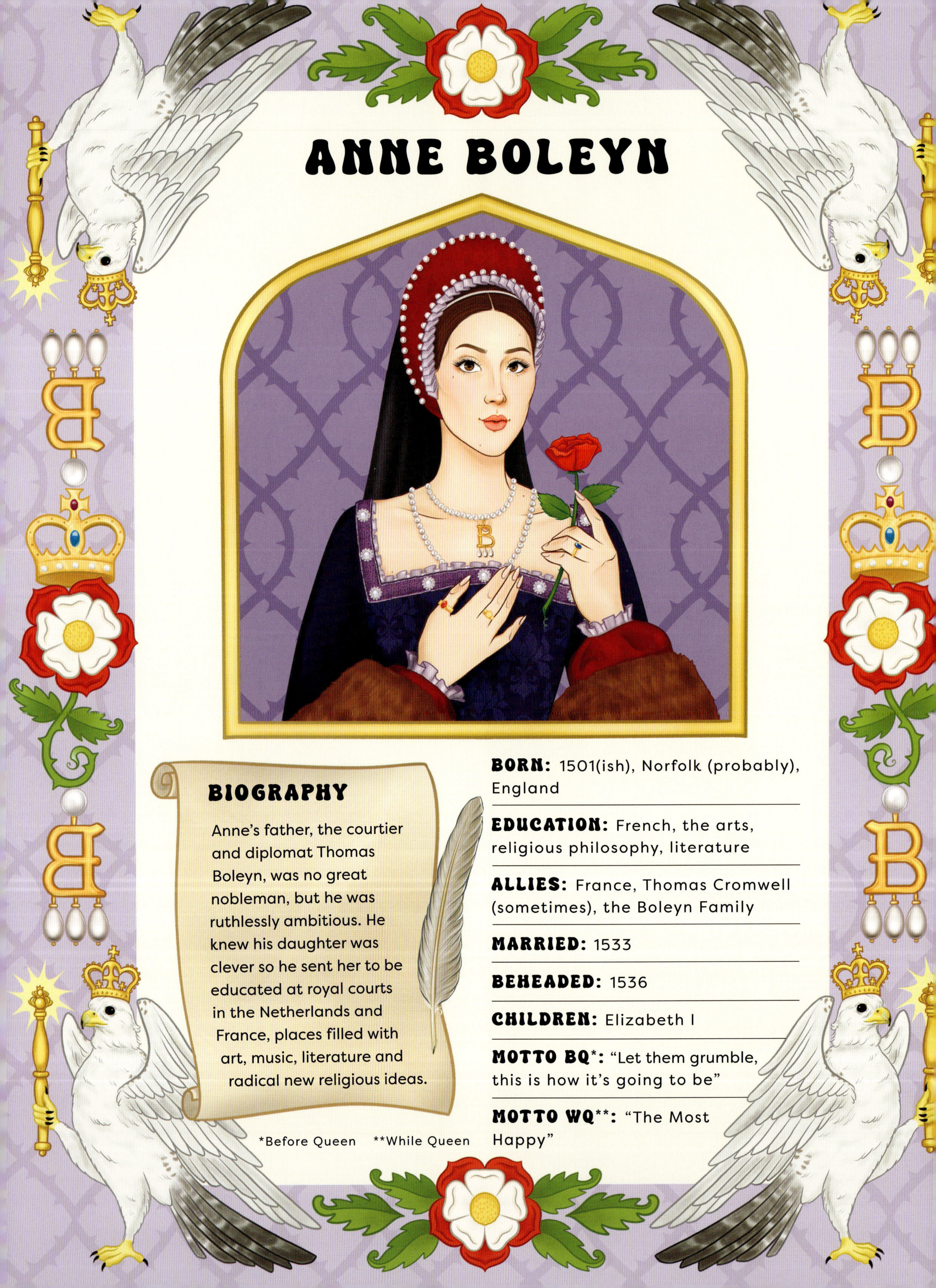

BIOGRAPHY

Anne's father, the courtier and diplomat Thomas Boleyn, was no great nobleman, but he was ruthlessly ambitious. He knew his daughter was clever so he sent her to be educated at royal courts in the Netherlands and France, places filled with art, music, literature and radical new religious ideas.

BORN: 1501(ish), Norfolk (probably), England

EDUCATION: French, the arts, religious philosophy, literature

ALLIES: France, Thomas Cromwell (sometimes), the Boleyn Family

MARRIED: 1533

BEHEADED: 1536

CHILDREN: Elizabeth I

MOTTO BQ*: "Let them grumble, this is how it's going to be"

MOTTO WQ:** "The Most Happy"

*Before Queen **While Queen

Court Superstar

Anne became a lady-in-waiting to Catherine of Aragon in 1522. She was glamorous, talented and extremely witty – she had undeniable STAR QUALITY.

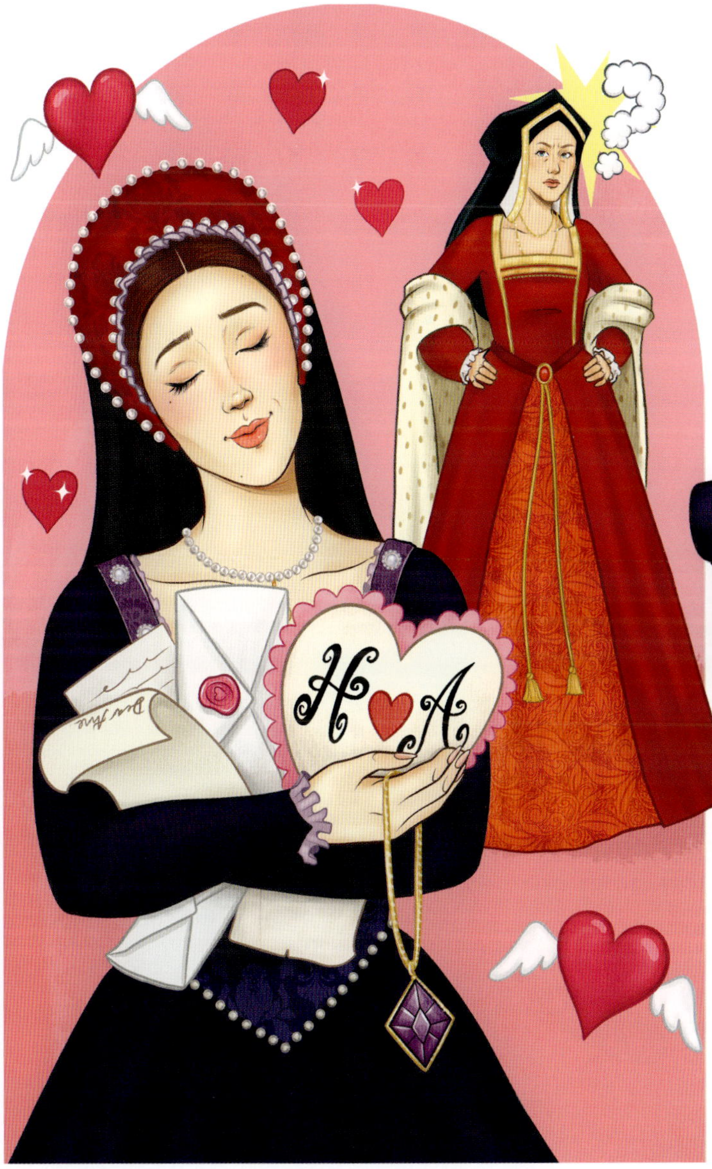
H A

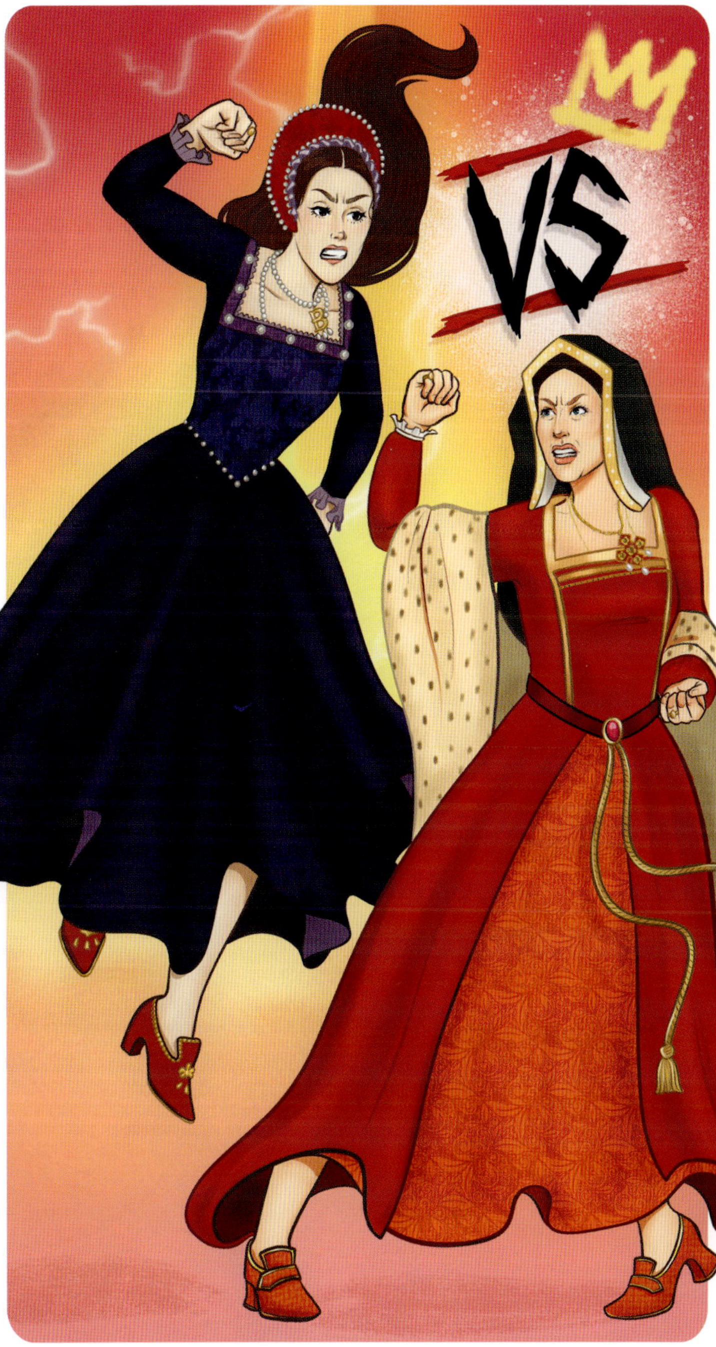
VS

King Henry fell head over heels in love. But he was still married to Catherine, who Anne worked for and *lived* with! He kept pursuing Anne – sending her jewels and lovelorn letters with doodles of their initials in hearts – until *eventually* she agreed to marry him. If he could get rid of Catherine . . .

Anne obtained land, titles and palaces, and created a powerful network of allies. Soon, people didn't know who to pay their respects to: Queen Catherine or Queen-To-Be Anne. Finally, in January 1533, Anne and Henry got married – but it was TOP SECRET because Henry was still officially married to Catherine!

Radical Religion

During the Tudor period, people had radical new ideas about religion. Anne was exposed to these opinions in Europe, and later she smuggled in books banned by the English authorities for containing 'dangerous' ideas.

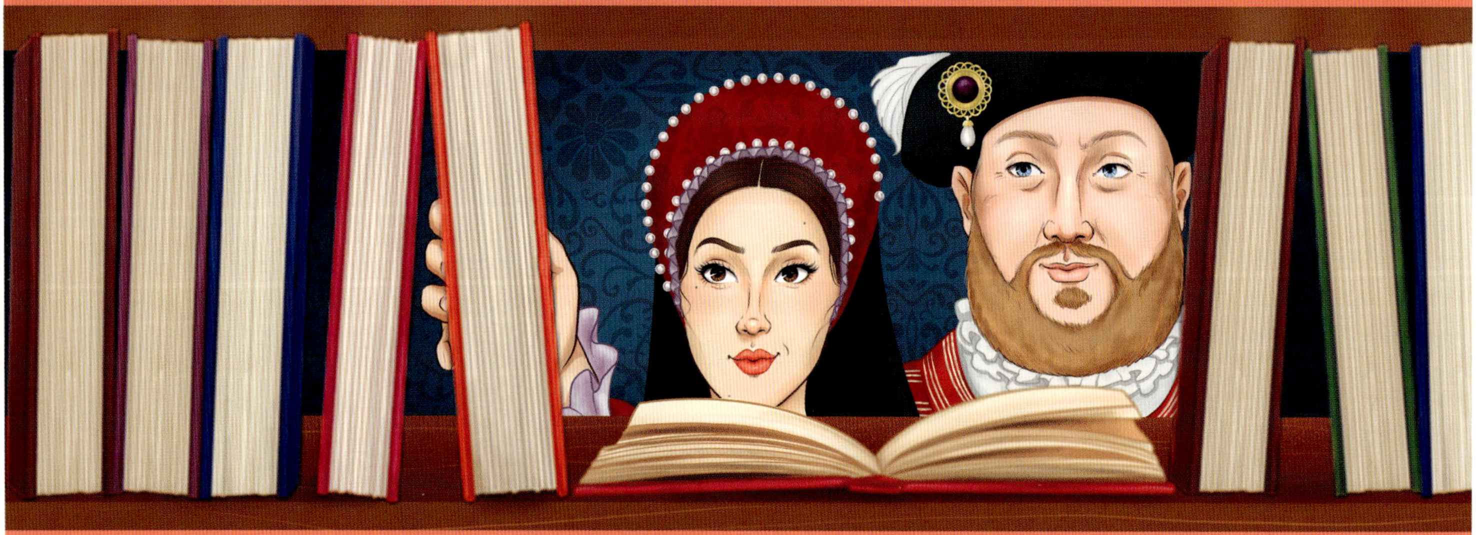

She showed some of these illegal books to the King – their ideas helped him come up with a plan to create the Church of England.

Not ANOTHER Girl

In September 1533 Anne had a baby GIRL – the future Queen Elizabeth I. Anne and Henry had hoped for a son and letters had already been written announcing the birth of a 'Prince'.

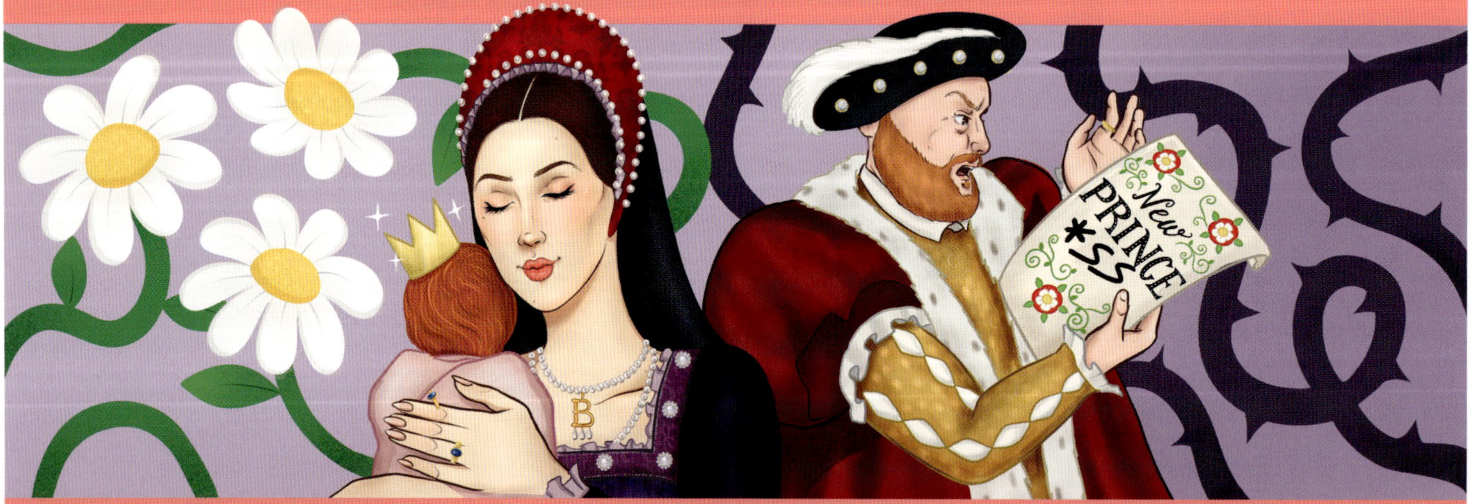
New
PRINCE
*SS

An extra 'ss' had to be added before they were sent out and Henry began to wonder if Anne had been the right wife for him after all.

Anne vs Cromwell

Thomas Cromwell, Henry VIII's most powerful advisor, was Anne's ally until they argued in 1535. Cromwell wanted to shut down the monasteries and send their riches to the royal treasuries. Anne thought the monasteries should be turned into schools and their wealth given to charity.

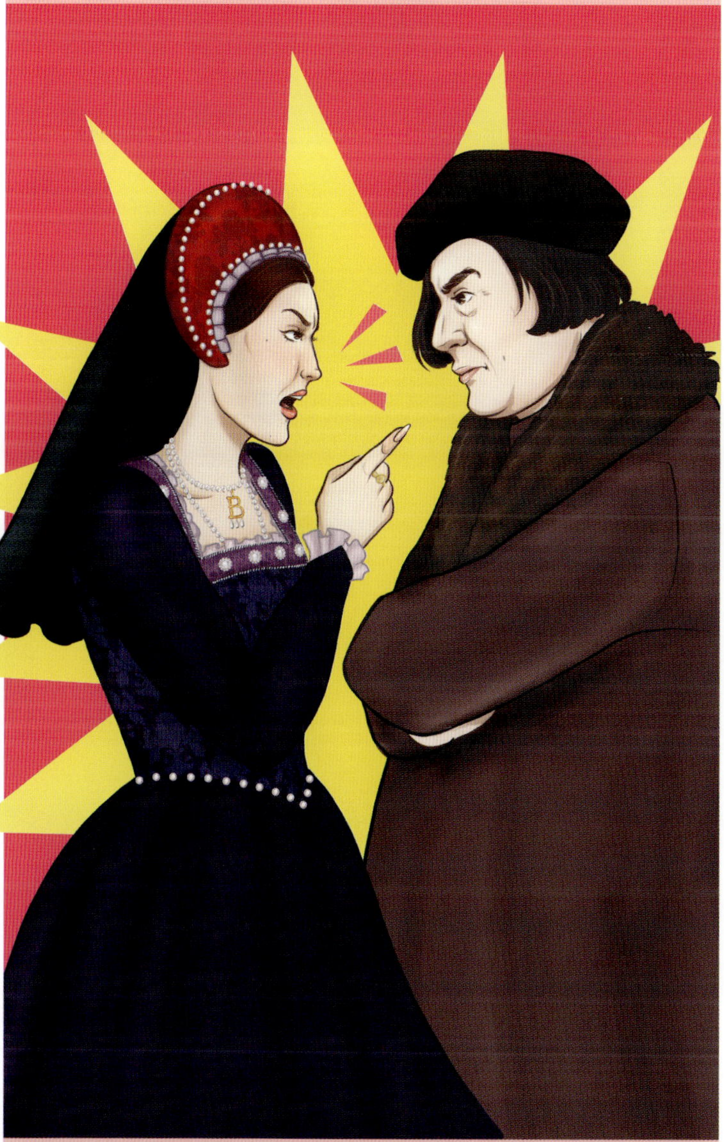

Their rows got so heated that Anne told Cromwell she'd 'like to see his head off his shoulders'. *Ouch.*

To the Tower!

In 1536, Henry decided to get rid of Anne once and for all and Thomas Cromwell was more than happy to help. Anne was accused of planning to kill Henry and having five other boyfriends while she was married – *even including her own brother!*

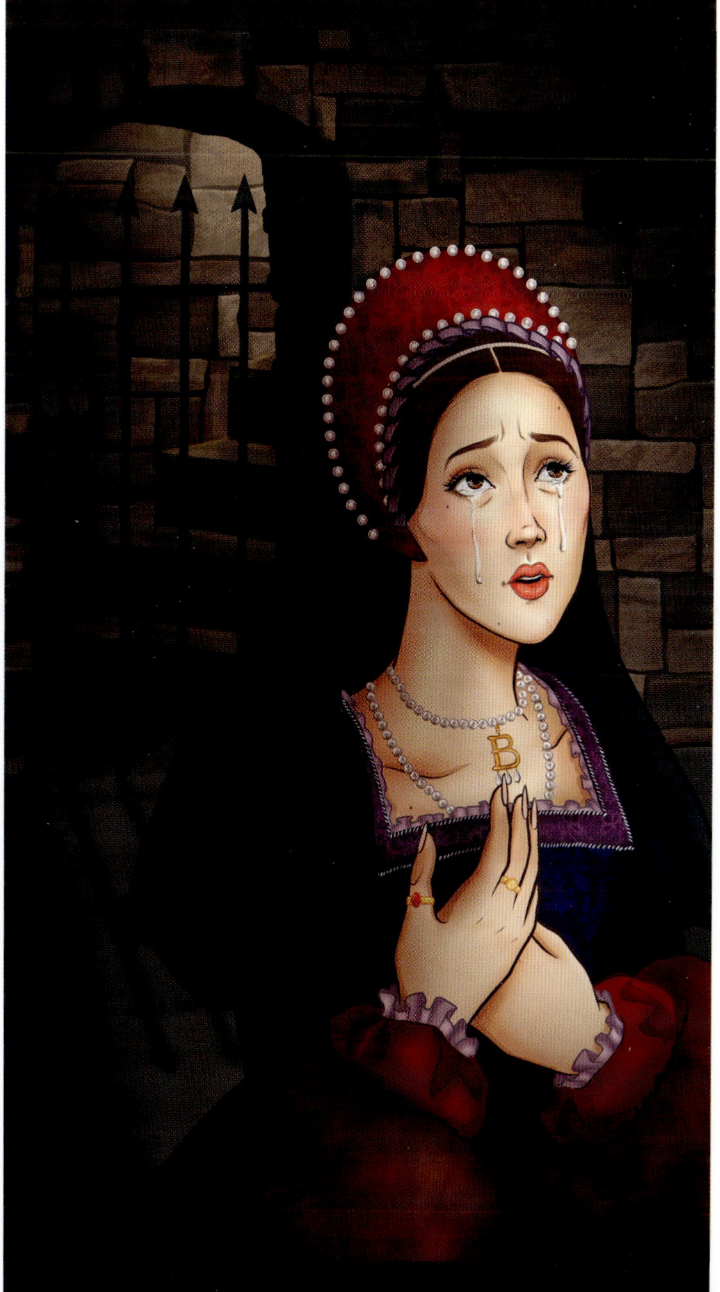

These charges were probably made up, but it didn't matter – the court did what Henry wanted and found Anne guilty, condemning her to execution.

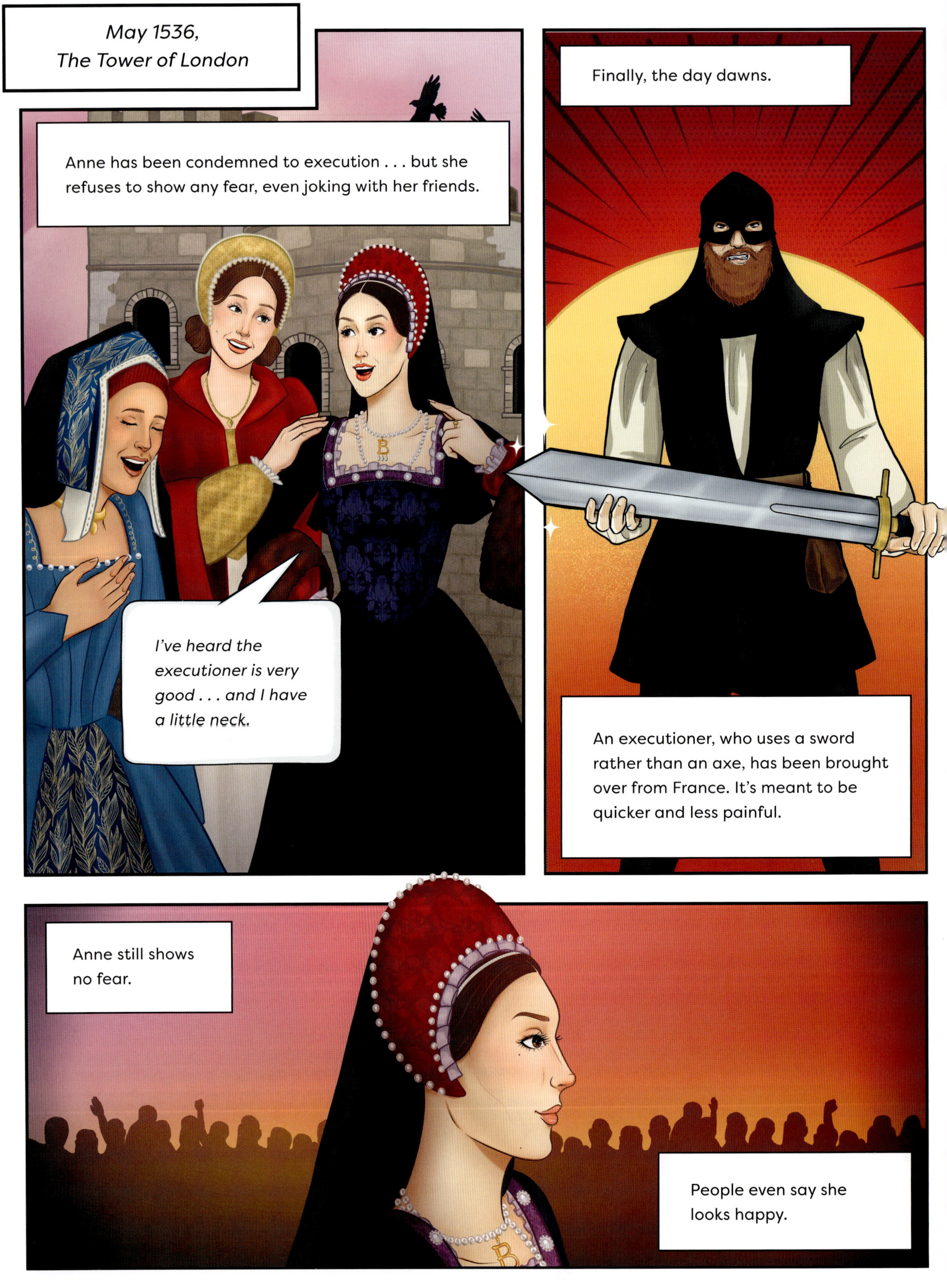
May 1536,
The Tower of London
Anne has been condemned to execution . . . but she refuses to show any fear, even joking with her friends.
I've heard the executioner is very good . . . and I have a little neck.
Finally, the day dawns.
An executioner, who uses a sword rather than an axe, has been brought over from France. It's meant to be quicker and less painful.
Anne still shows no fear.
People even say she looks happy.

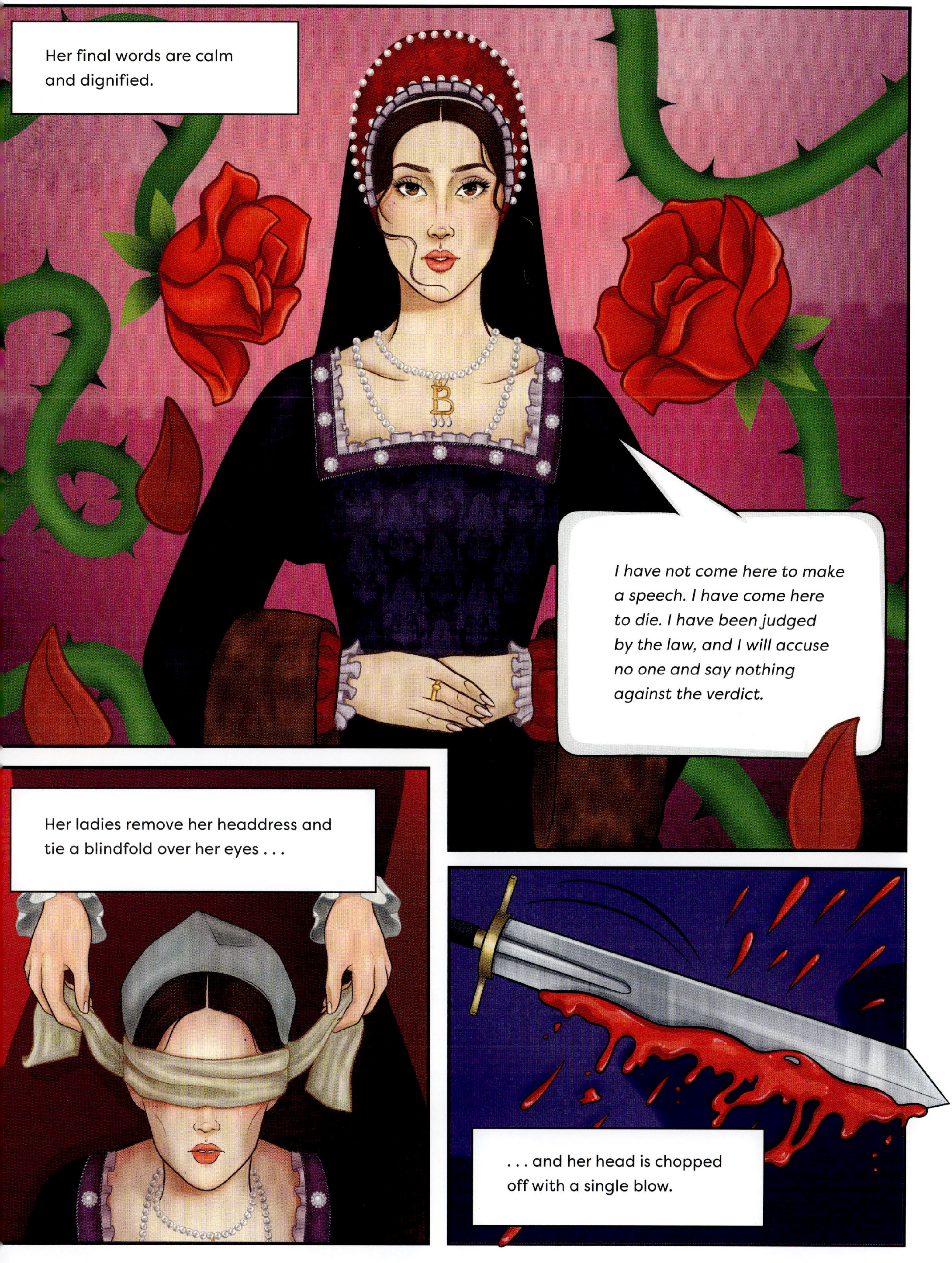
Her final words are calm and dignified.
I have not come here to make a speech. I have come here to die. I have been judged by the law, and I will accuse no one and say nothing against the verdict.
Her ladies remove her headdress and tie a blindfold over her eyes . . .
. . . and her head is chopped off with a single blow.

JANE SEYMOUR

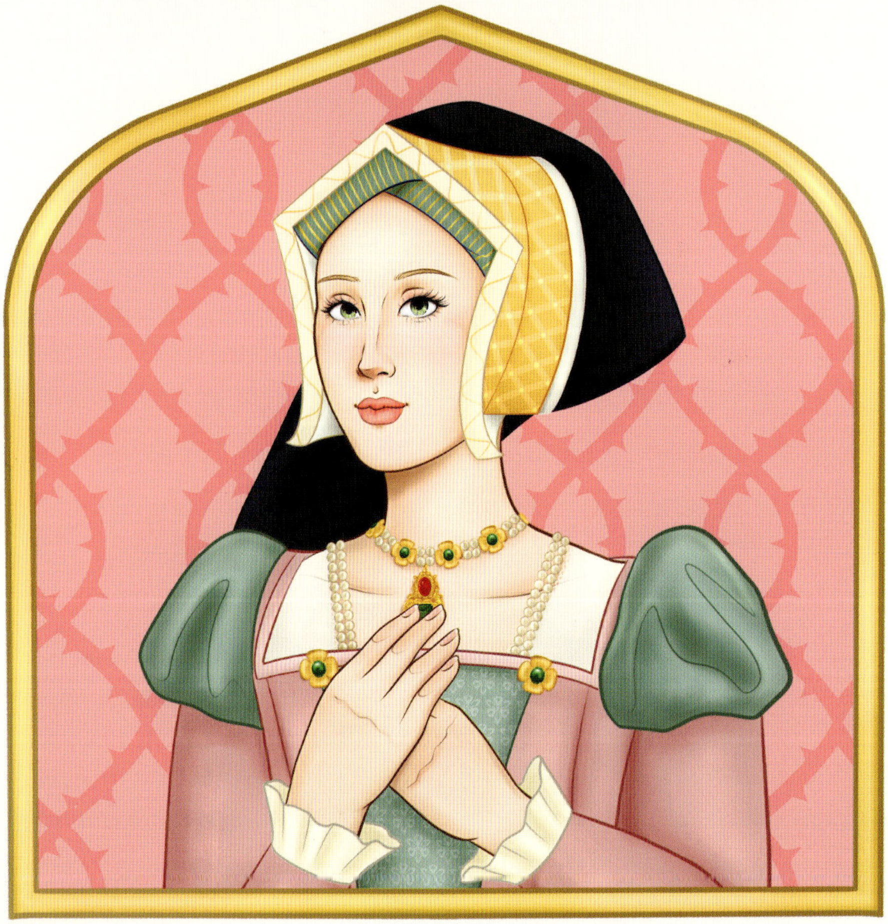

BIOGRAPHY

The Seymour family were on the rise. Jane became a lady-in-waiting to Catherine of Aragon. She witnessed the drama between Henry, Catherine and Anne Boleyn. Jane sympathised with Catherine, but she wanted to keep her place at court, so when Anne was crowned queen, Jane became Anne's lady-in-waiting.

BORN: 1508(ish), Wulfhall, Wiltshire, England

EDUCATION: Household management, embroidery, cookery, riding

ALLIES: The Seymour family, the Holy Roman Emperor, Princess Mary

MARRIED: 1536

DIED: 1537

CHILDREN: Edward VI

MOTTO: "Bound to Obey and Serve"

A Woman of Honour

People at court started to notice that Henry fancied Jane while he was still married to Anne Boleyn. Jane was known to be kind, gentle and loyal, and they hoped she might calm down the dramatic Tudor court. At first glance she seemed meek and gentle, but she was also ambitious and determined.

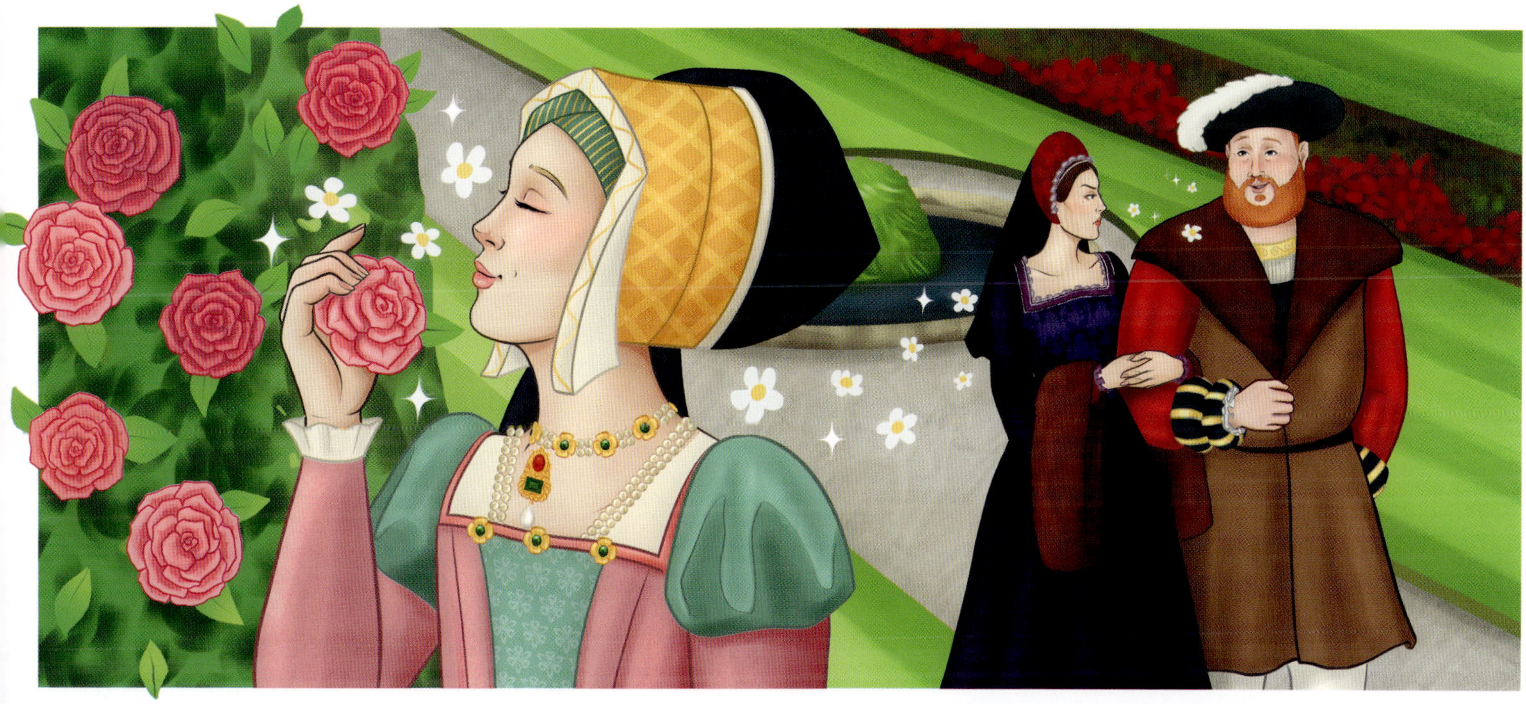

When Henry sent Jane a present of gold coins, she sent them straight back to him: he was still married, and she said she'd rather die a thousand times than risk her honour. Her plan worked and Henry became more determined than ever to get rid of Anne and marry Jane.

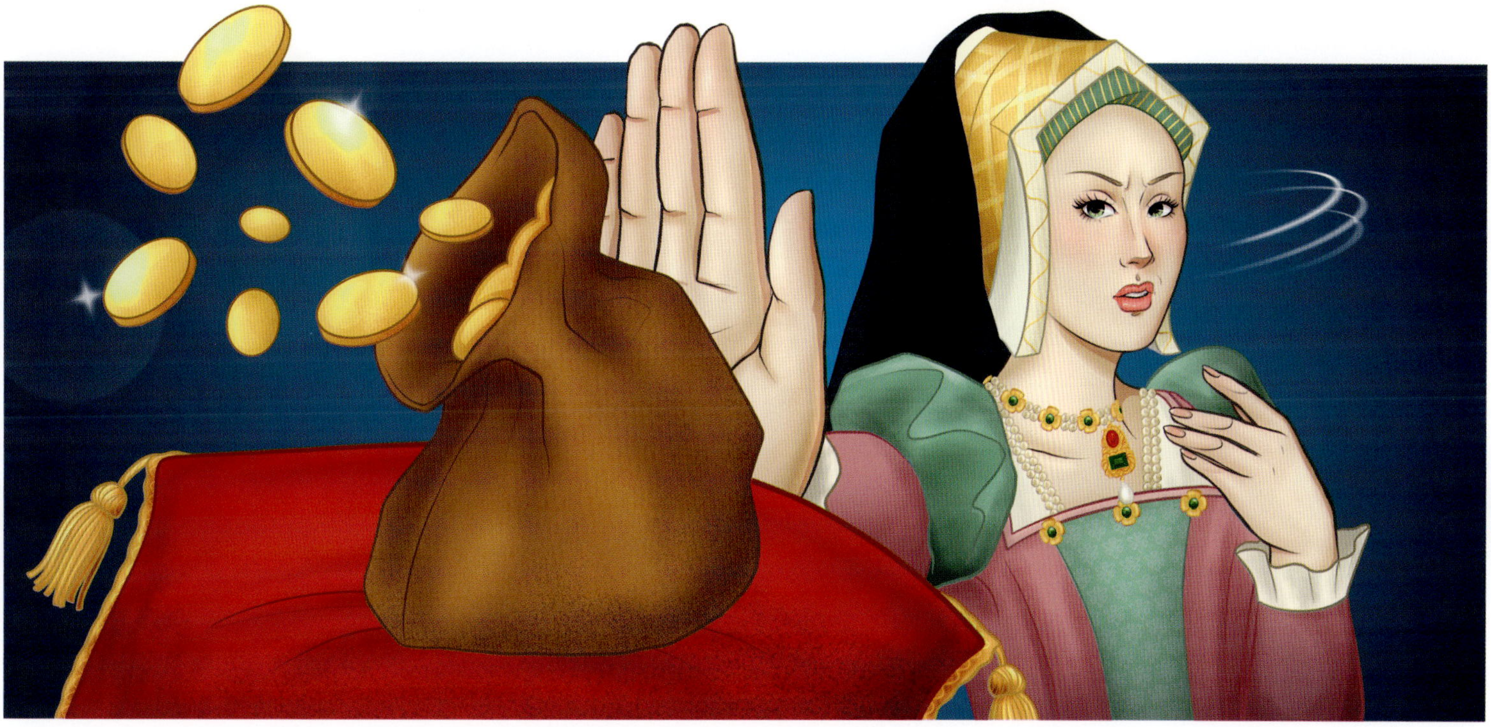

Give it a Day

As soon as Henry heard that Anne's execution had taken place, he rushed to be with Jane – they got engaged less than a day after Anne's head had been chopped off!

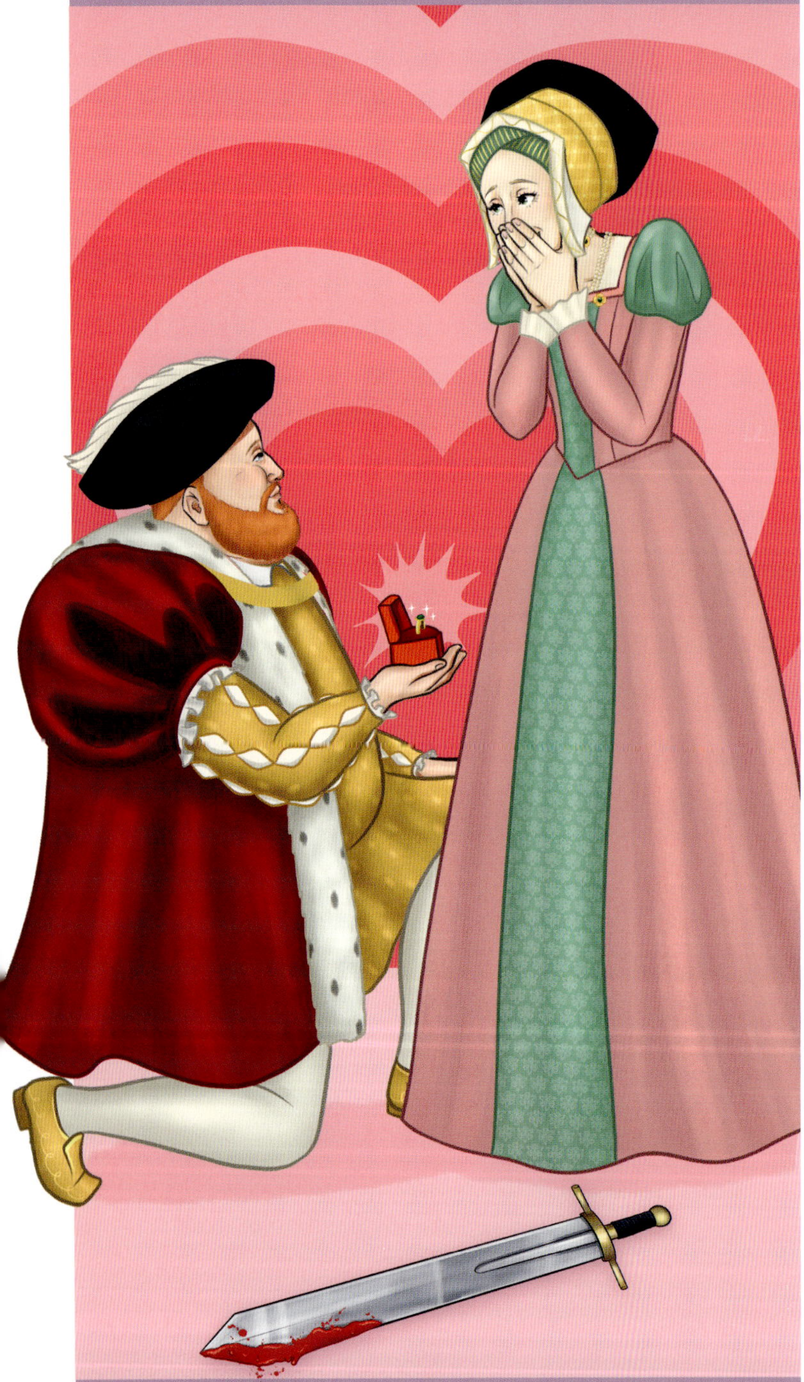

Before long they were married. Henry gave his new wife 104 country estates as a wedding present!

Stepmother of the Year

When Henry divorced Catherine, he also disowned their daughter Mary. Jane had become close to Mary – who was only eight years younger than her! – when she worked for Catherine, and now she made it her mission to rebuild the relationship between father and daughter.

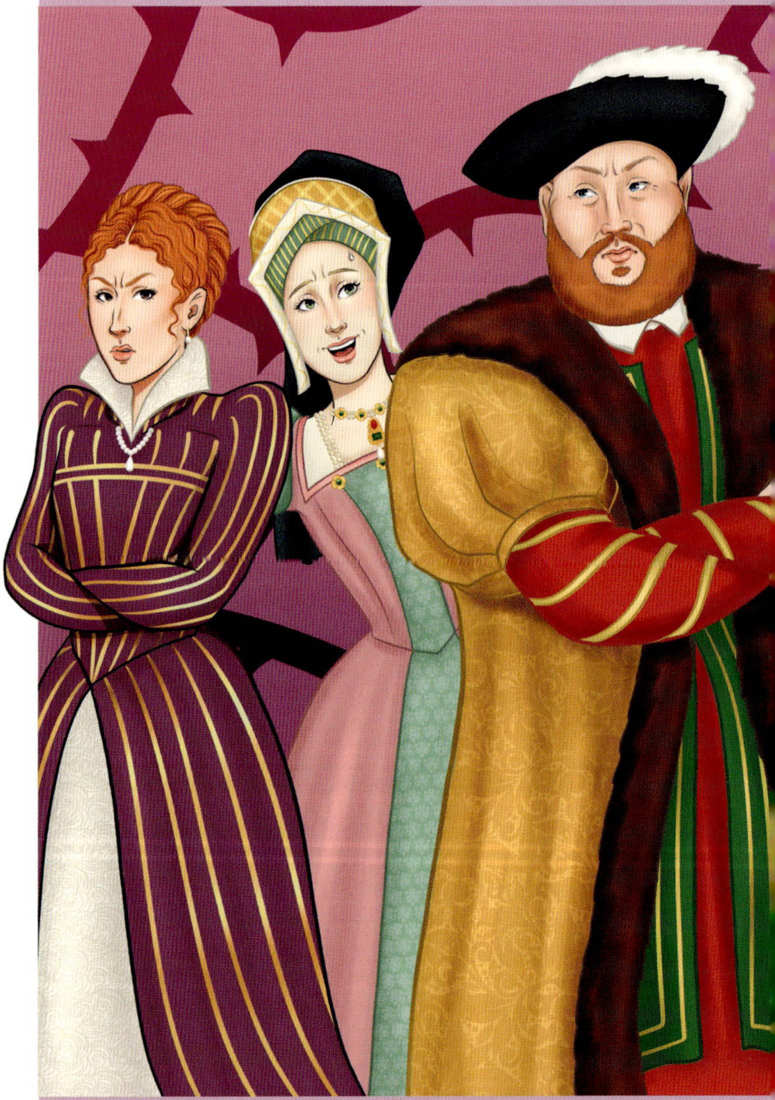

At first, Henry flew into a rage whenever she raised the issue, but Jane kept trying and eventually she persuaded her husband to make up with his daughter and bring her to live with them.

Fashion Wars

Jane knew her best chance of survival was to play the quiet and obedient wife, so she found other ways of making her voice heard. Anne had made French styles of dress popular at court, especially the French Hood, a headdress which showed the front of the hair – scandalous!

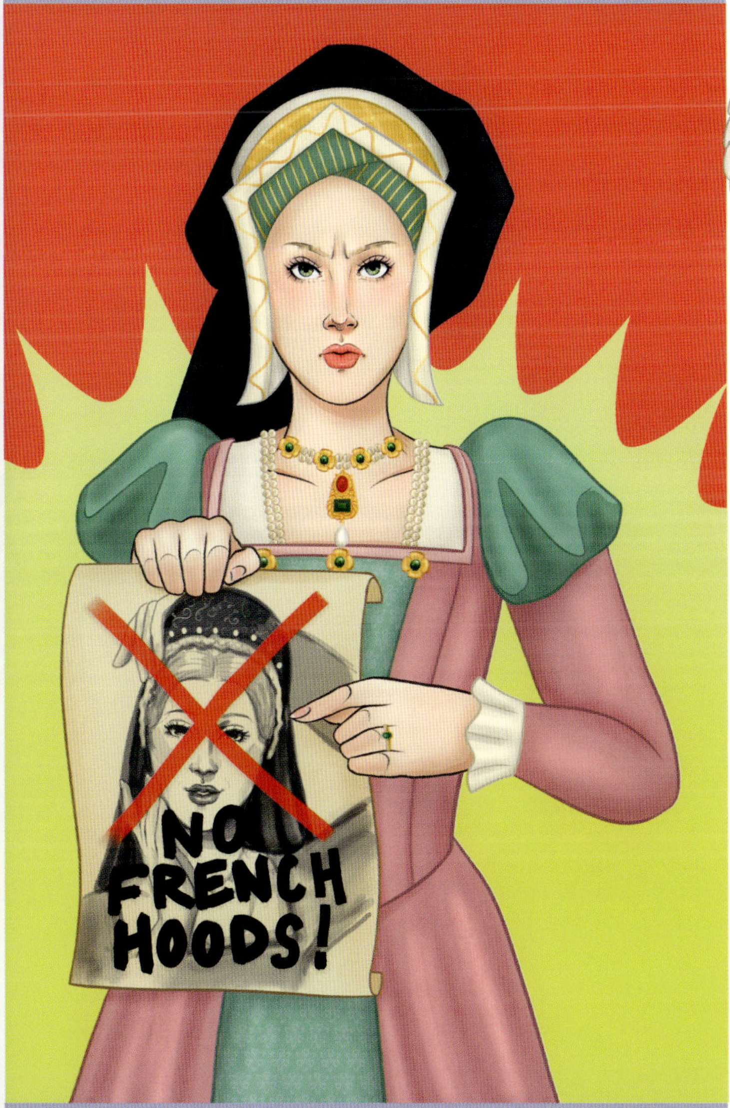
NO FRENCH HOODS!

Jane banned her ladies from wearing these fashions. By going back to traditional English styles, Jane was announcing she was different to Anne and promising to be a loyal queen of England.

It's a Boy!

In October 1537 Jane gave birth to a son, Edward – *finally!* The royal couple and the whole country were overjoyed but childbirth in Tudor times was dangerous for mothers as well as babies.

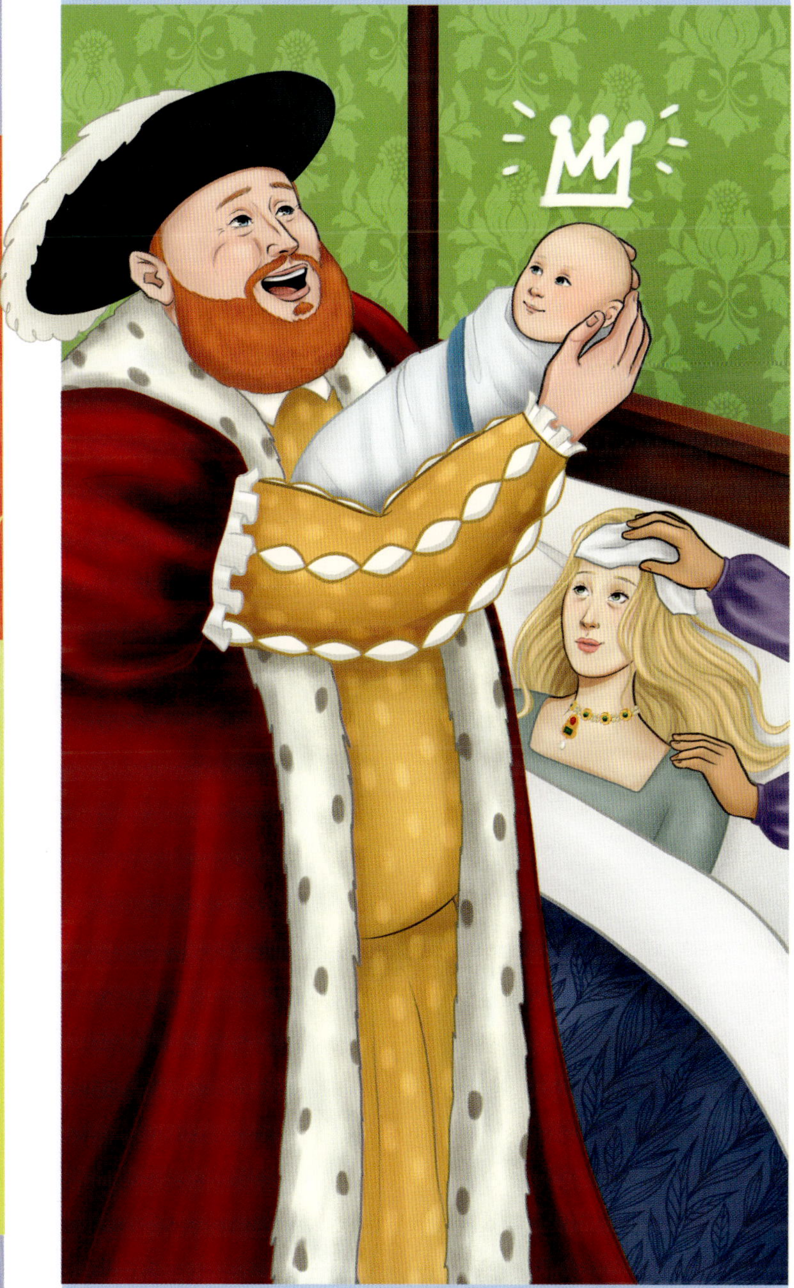

Jane became ill and died less than two weeks after her son was born. She is the only one of Henry's wives who was buried beside him – she was the favourite because she gave him a son.

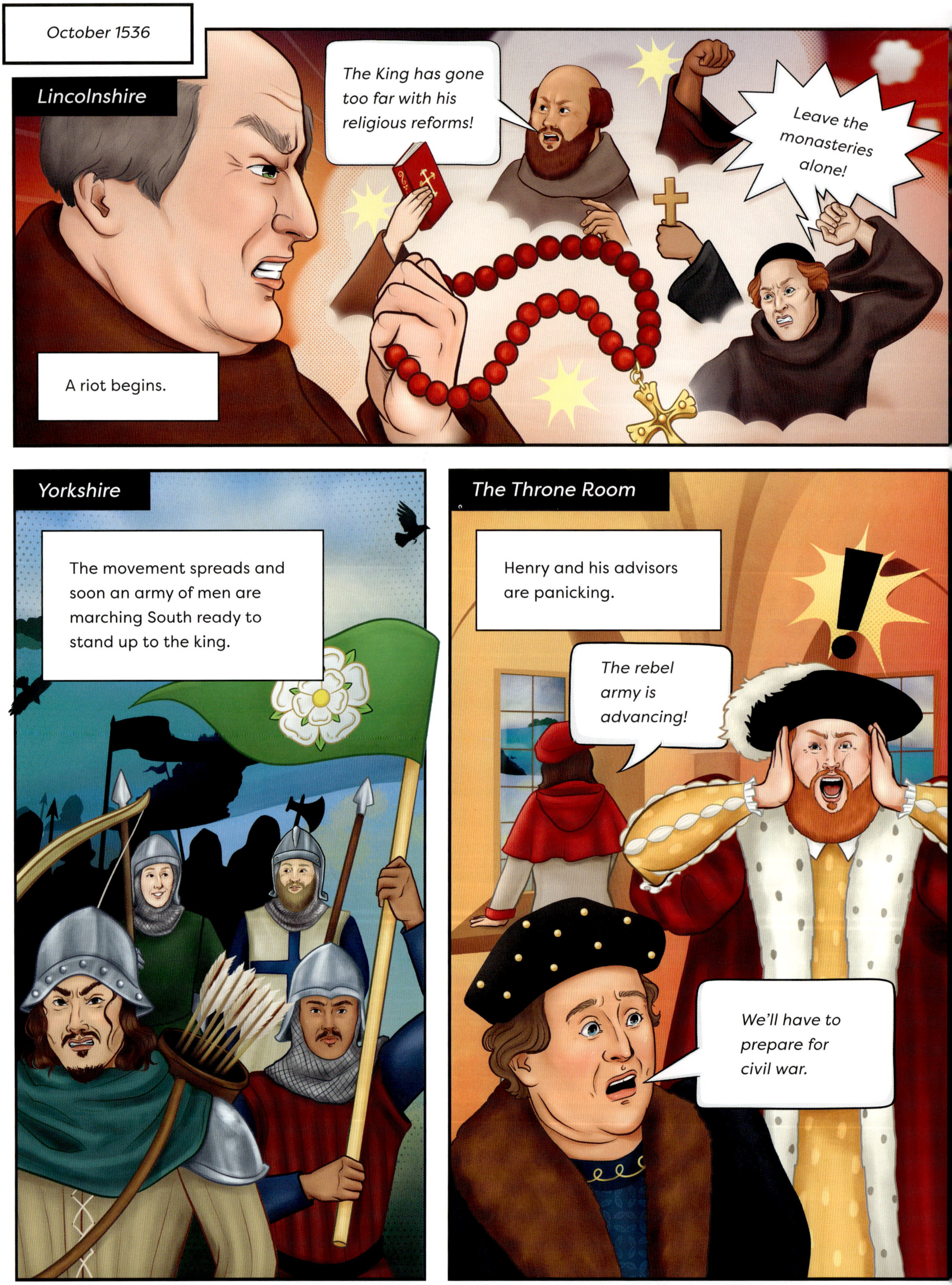
October 1536
Lincolnshire
The King has gone too far with his religious reforms!
Leave the monasteries alone!
A riot begins.
Yorkshire
The movement spreads and soon an army of men are marching South ready to stand up to the king.
The Throne Room
Henry and his advisors are panicking.
The rebel army is advancing!
We'll have to prepare for civil war.

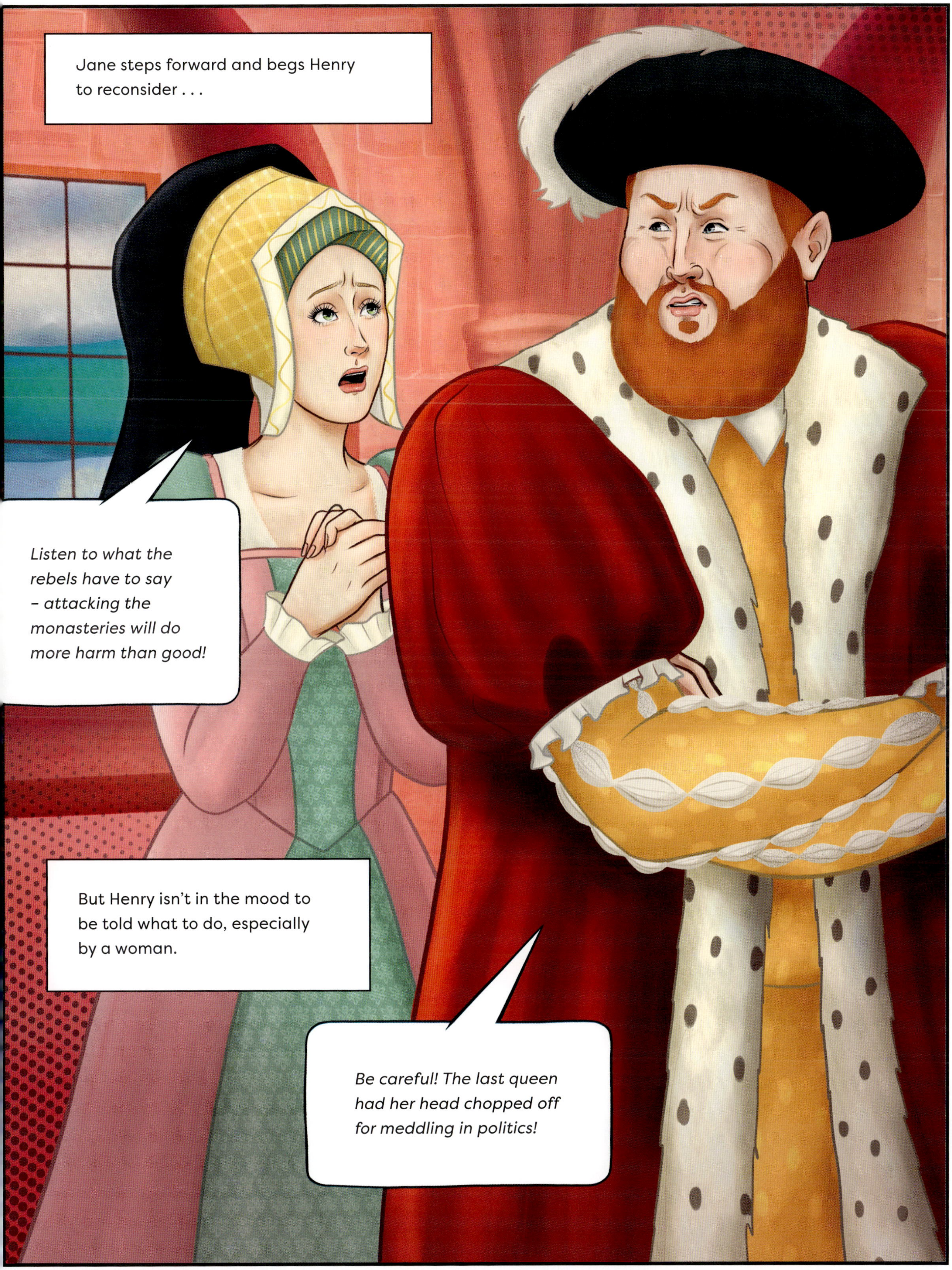
Jane steps forward and begs Henry to reconsider . . .
Listen to what the rebels have to say – attacking the monasteries will do more harm than good!
But Henry isn't in the mood to be told what to do, especially by a woman.
Be careful! The last queen had her head chopped off for meddling in politics!

ANNE OF CLEVES

BIOGRAPHY

Anne (or Anna as she was known in her homeland) was the daughter of the duke of Cleves, a small kingdom in what is now Germany. After Jane Seymour died, Henry tasked Thomas Cromwell with finding him a new bride. Anne seemed perfect – her brother-in-law was the powerful ruler of Saxony and her brother William ruled Cleves, which, like England, had left the Catholic Church.

BORN: 1515, Cleves, Germany

EDUCATION: Reading and writing, embroidery, cooking, card games

ALLIES: The Duke of Cleves, The Protestant Confederation of Germany, Thomas Cromwell

MARRIED: 1540

DIVORCED: 1540

DIED: 1557

CHILDREN: None

MOTTO: "God Send Me Well to Keep"

Culture Shock

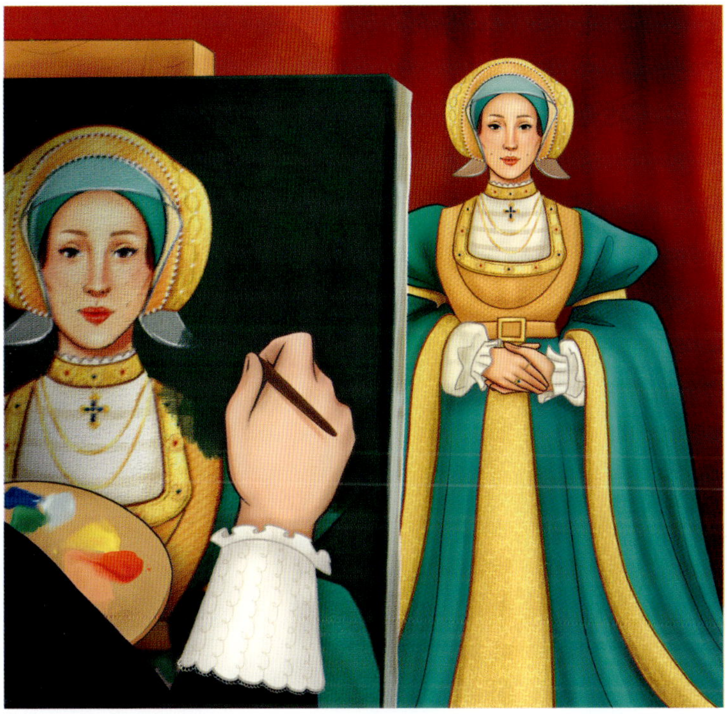

Hans Holbein, the English court painter, was sent to paint Anne's picture.

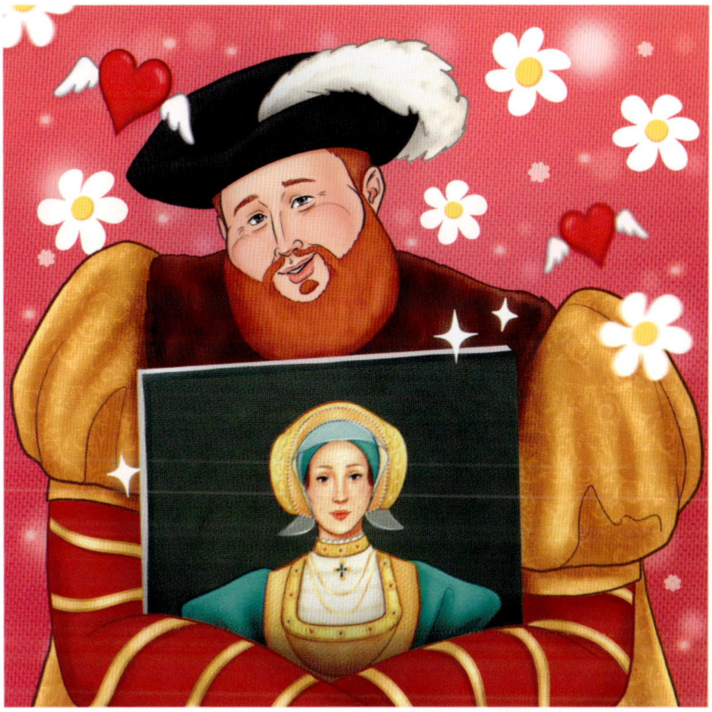

Henry fell in love with the painting and Anne was sent to England.

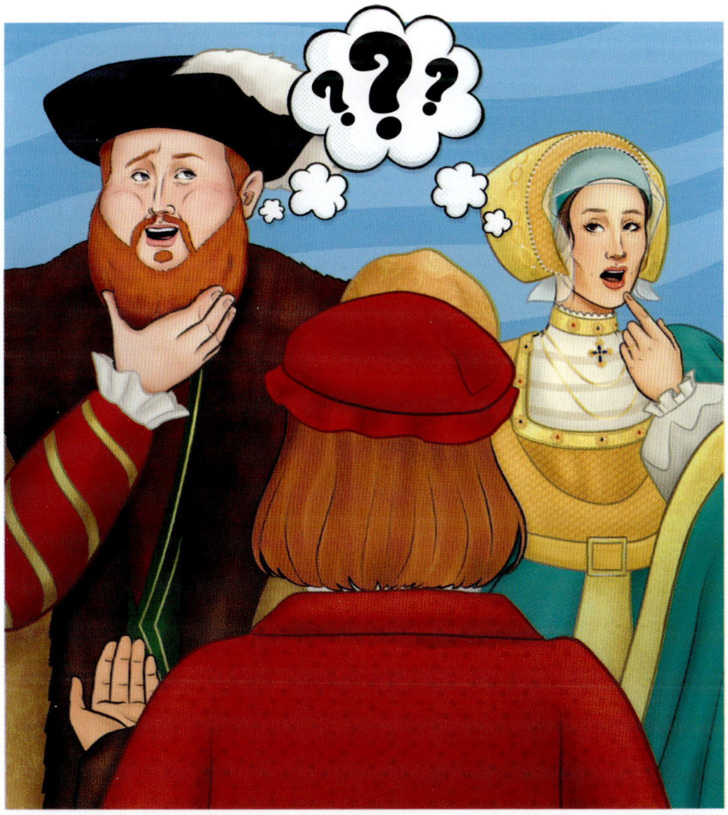
???

Anne didn't speak English, and although she was clever and learning quickly, she'd still need an interpreter for the first months of her marriage.

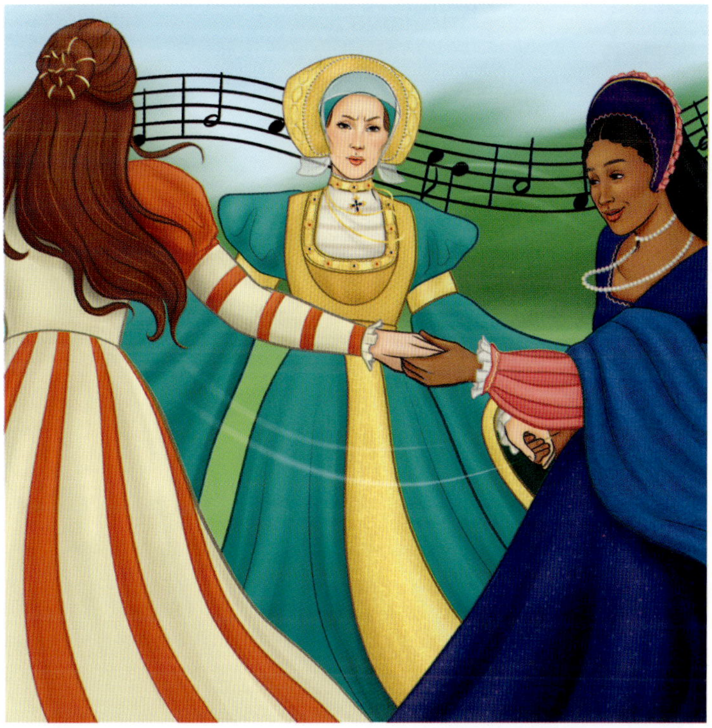

English culture was very different too: in Cleves the men and women lived quite separately, and women didn't dance, sing, or take part in the pageants that were so important to Henry and the English court.

A Short Marriage

Anne did everything she could to prepare for her new role. During her journey to England, she ate with the English men and even asked to be taught one of Henry's favourite card games so that the two would have something to do together.

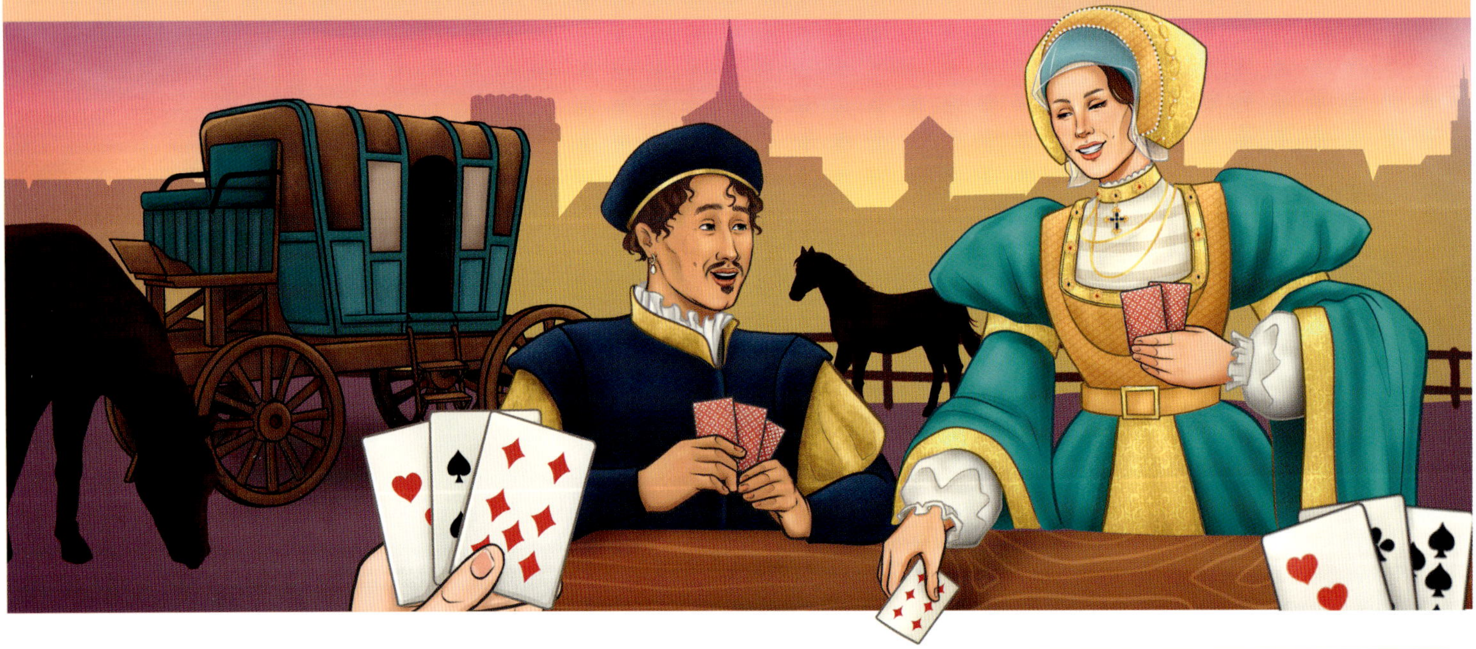

Despite all her efforts, Henry and Anne's first meeting went disastrously, and things never improved. Henry claimed not to find Anne attractive, and the politics of the alliance with her brother William of Cleves were looking increasingly risky.

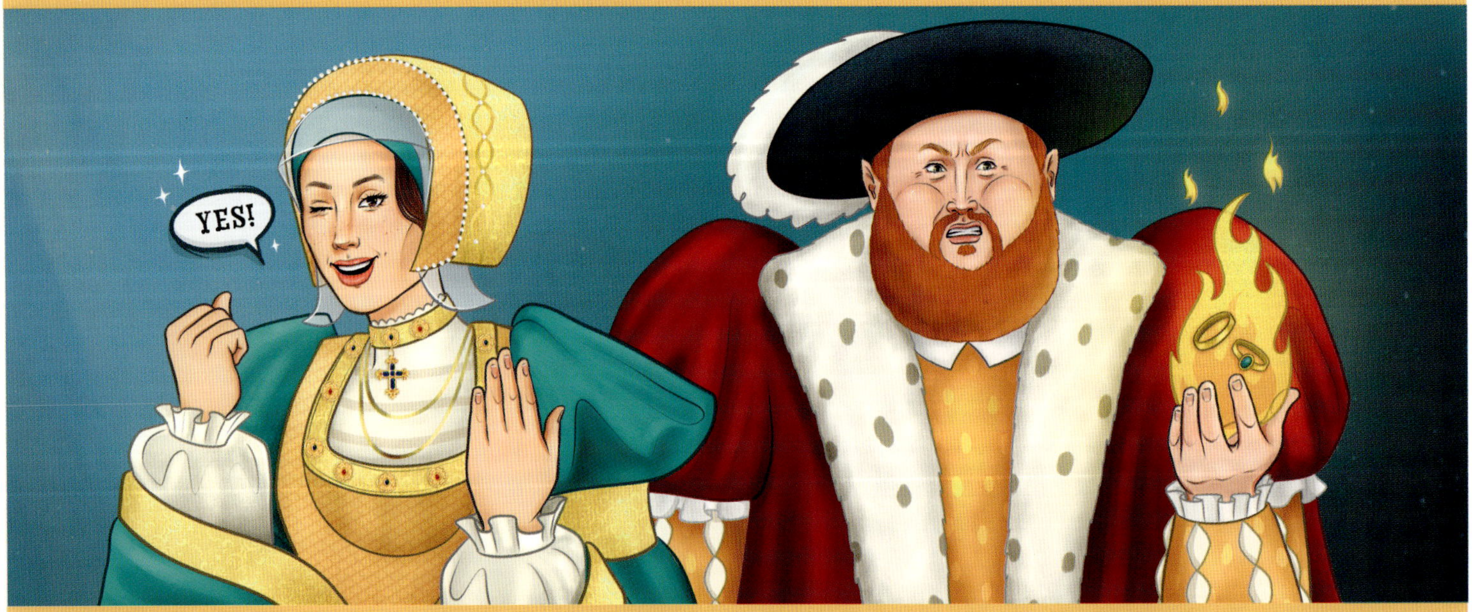
YES!

Six months after their wedding Henry demanded an annulment. Cleverly (and – let's be real – *perhaps happily!*) Anne agreed.

The King's Sister

After their divorce, Anne stayed in England. Henry gave her two palaces and lots of land, as well as furniture, art, jewels and servants. Henry promised that she would always be welcome at court and that from now on she'd be known as 'the king's beloved sister'.

Now Anne had a huge income and was free to live as she pleased. She hunted in her forests, cooked traditional German food and went to court whenever she fancied it.

The Friendly Wives' Club

The first time Anne visited court after her divorce, her successor, Catherine Howard, was nervous that things would be awkward. Anne, however, was determined that they wouldn't be.

One evening, the three had dinner together. Anne and Catherine got on so well that the two stayed up chatting long after Henry had gone to bed!

Anne outlived Henry and was given a magnificent burial in Westminster Cathedral by her former stepdaughter Mary I.

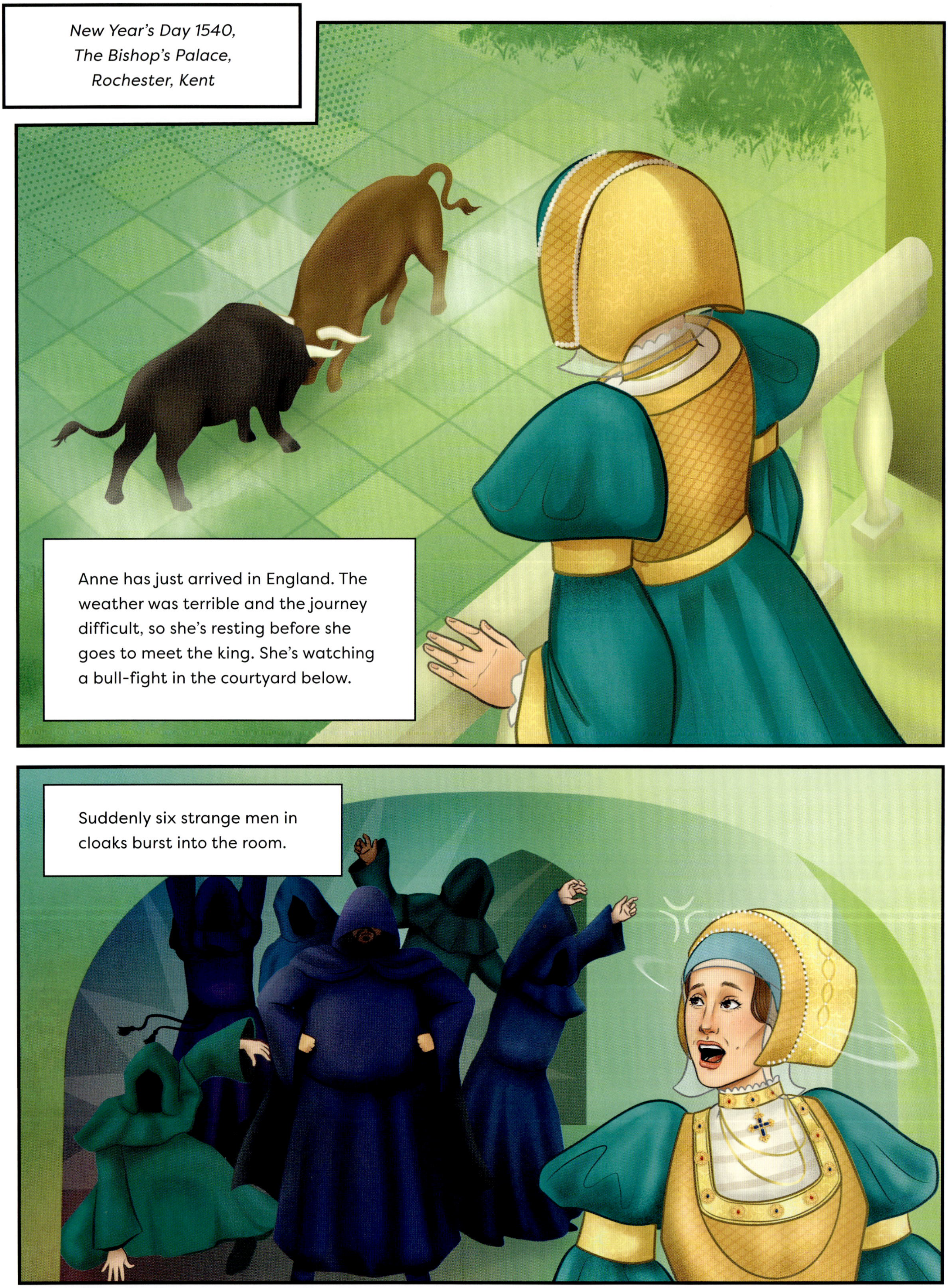
New Year's Day 1540,
The Bishop's Palace,
Rochester, Kent
Anne has just arrived in England. The weather was terrible and the journey difficult, so she's resting before she goes to meet the king. She's watching a bull-fight in the courtyard below.
Suddenly six strange men in cloaks burst into the room.

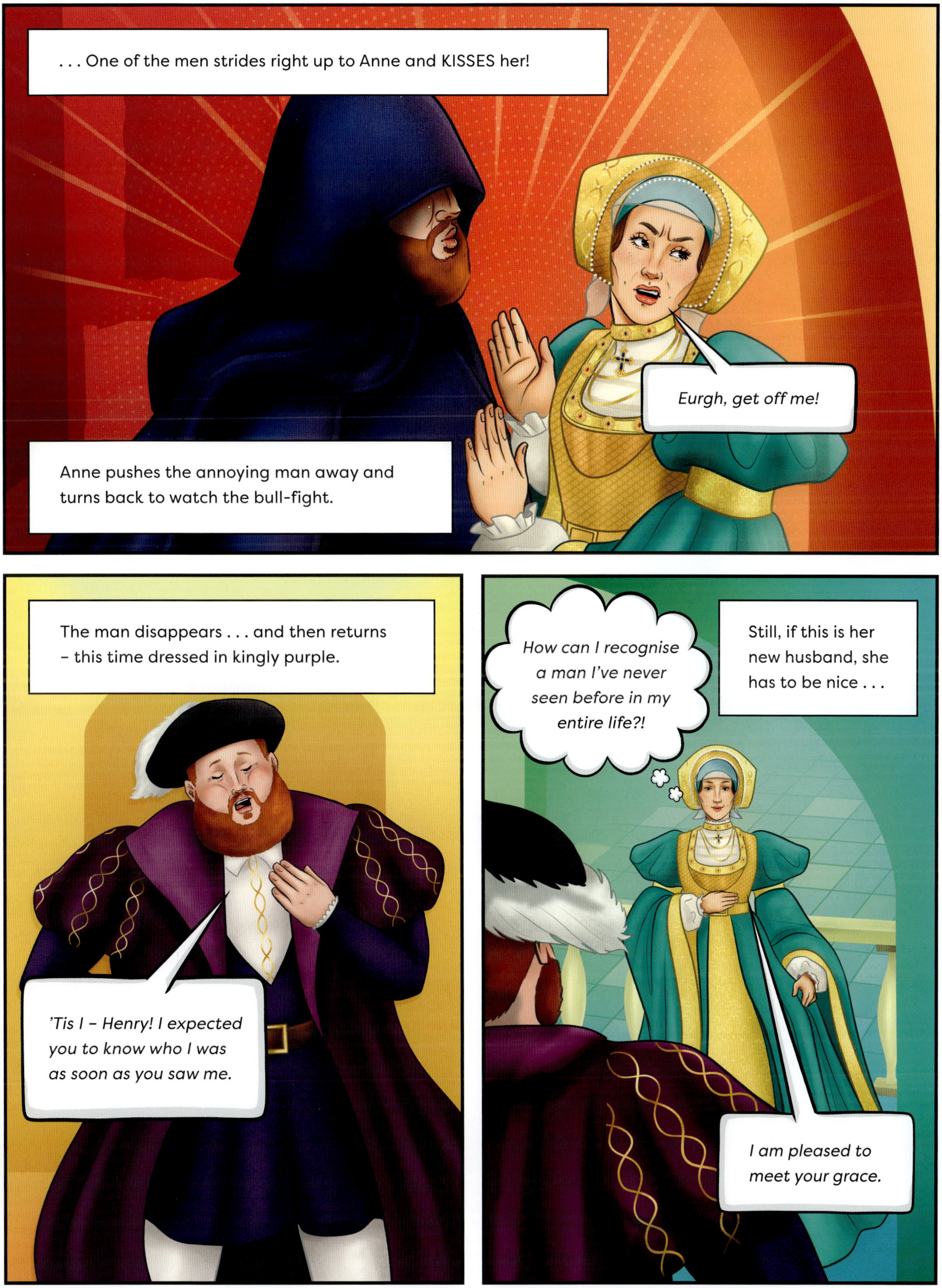
. . . One of the men strides right up to Anne and KISSES her!
Eurgh, get off me!
Anne pushes the annoying man away and turns back to watch the bull-fight.
The man disappears . . . and then returns – this time dressed in kingly purple.
'Tis I – Henry! I expected you to know who I was as soon as you saw me.
How can I recognise a man I've never seen before in my entire life?!
Still, if this is her new husband, she has to be nice . . .
I am pleased to meet your grace.

CATHERINE HOWARD

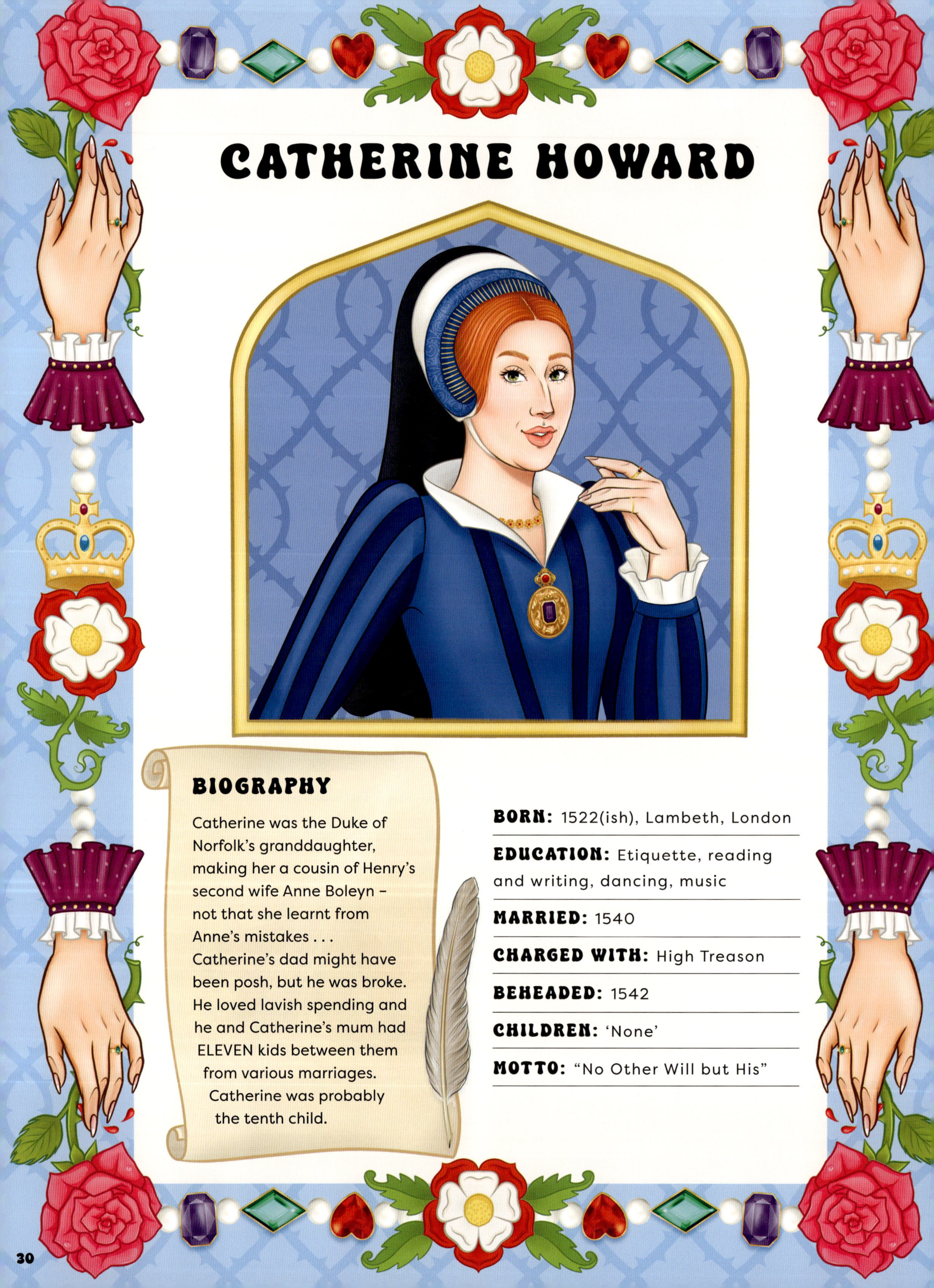

BIOGRAPHY

Catherine was the Duke of Norfolk's granddaughter, making her a cousin of Henry's second wife Anne Boleyn – not that she learnt from Anne's mistakes . . . Catherine's dad might have been posh, but he was broke. He loved lavish spending and he and Catherine's mum had ELEVEN kids between them from various marriages. Catherine was probably the tenth child.

BORN: 1522(ish), Lambeth, London

EDUCATION: Etiquette, reading and writing, dancing, music

MARRIED: 1540

CHARGED WITH: High Treason

BEHEADED: 1542

CHILDREN: 'None'

MOTTO: "No Other Will but His"

Girls Just Want to Have Fun

Catherine was sent to be raised by her step-grandmother, the powerful Dowager Duchess of Norfolk. It sounds strange to us, but it was quite normal for Tudor families to send their children to be educated in the households of wealthy relatives.

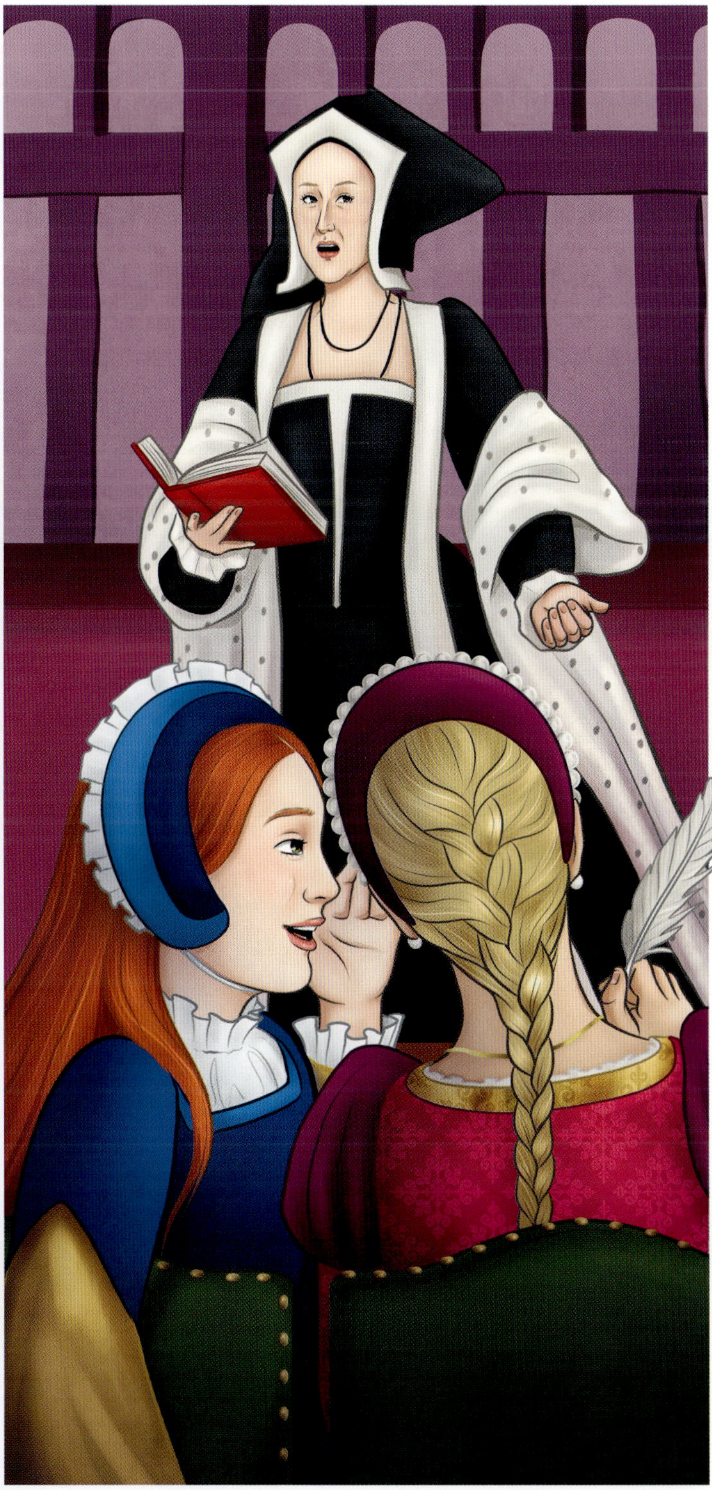

The Dowager Duchess' house was almost like a boarding school, with lots of teenagers sleeping in boys' and girls' dormitories.

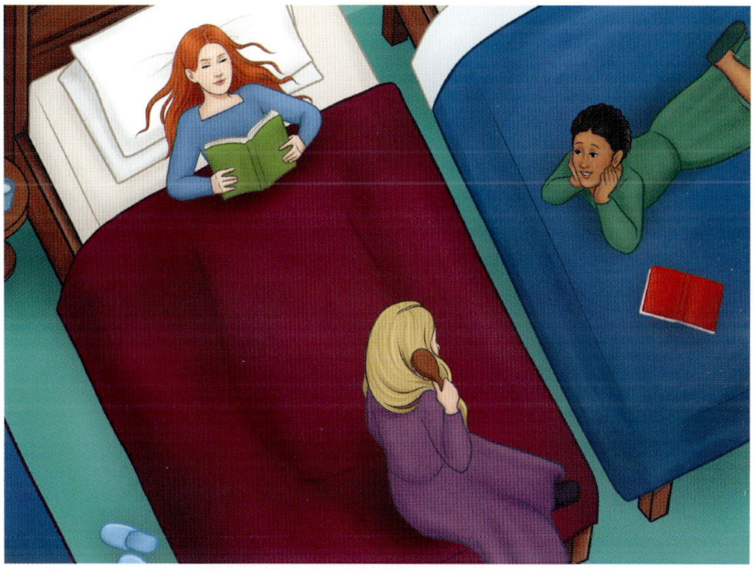

Everyone loved Catherine but she could be very naughty; she arranged wild midnight feasts and had two boyfriends. Catherine was just having fun, but it would come back to bite her once she was married to the king.

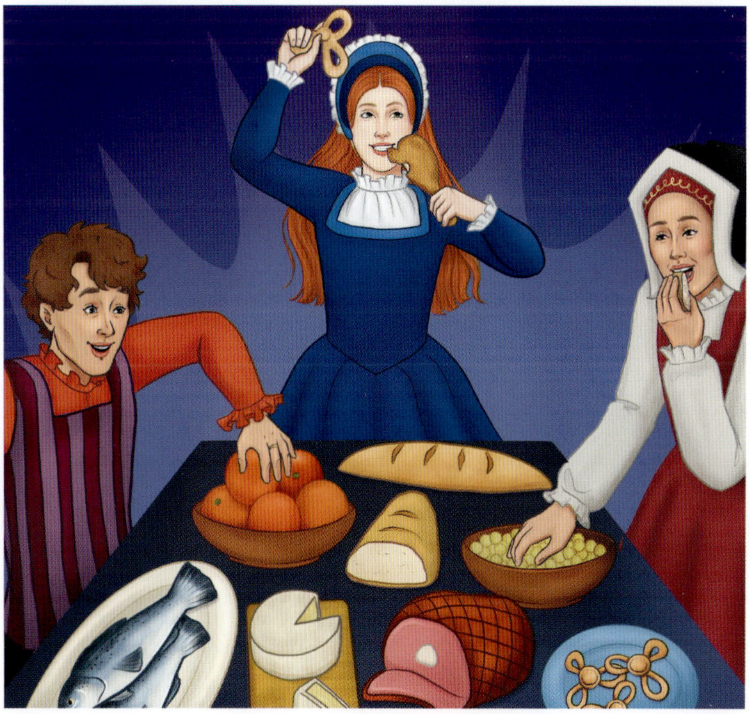

A Rose and a Thorn

When Henry married Anne of Cleves, Catherine Howard was made one of her ladies-in-waiting. Everyone at court noticed her – she was beautiful, elegant and most of all, *fun*. Henry decided he HAD to marry her!

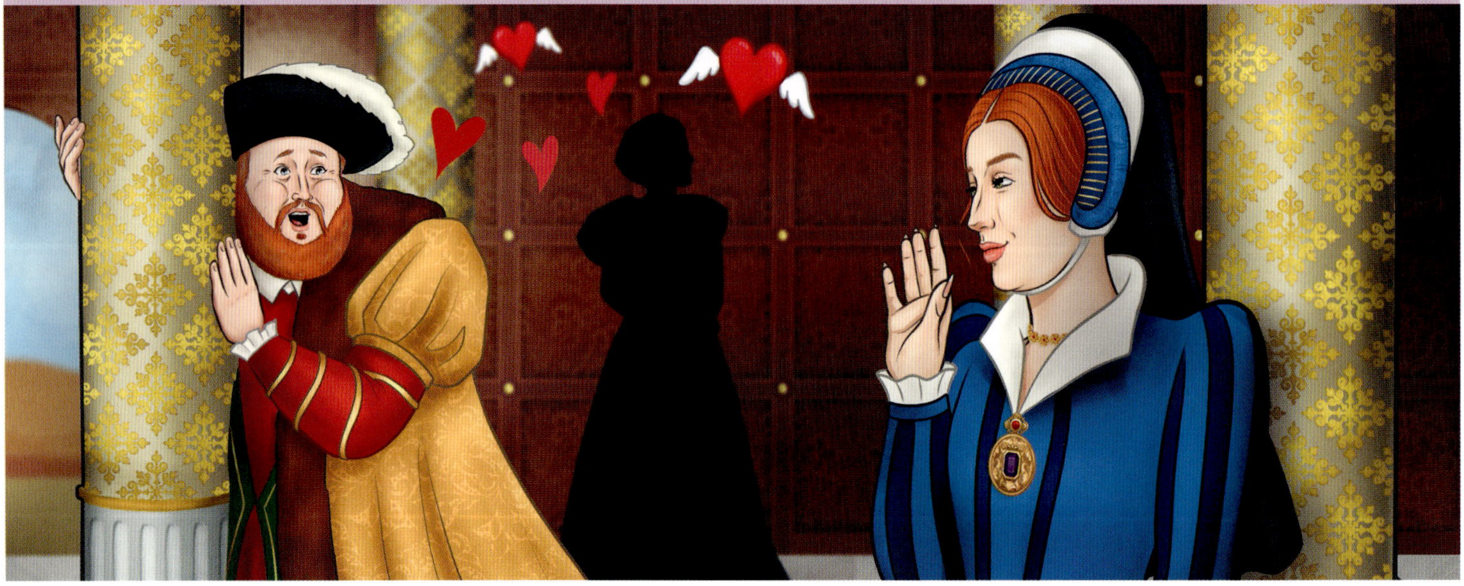

Henry and Catherine got married less than three weeks after he divorced Anne. Catherine was his 'jewel of womanhood' and his 'rose without a thorn'. She might have felt slightly differently about him . . .

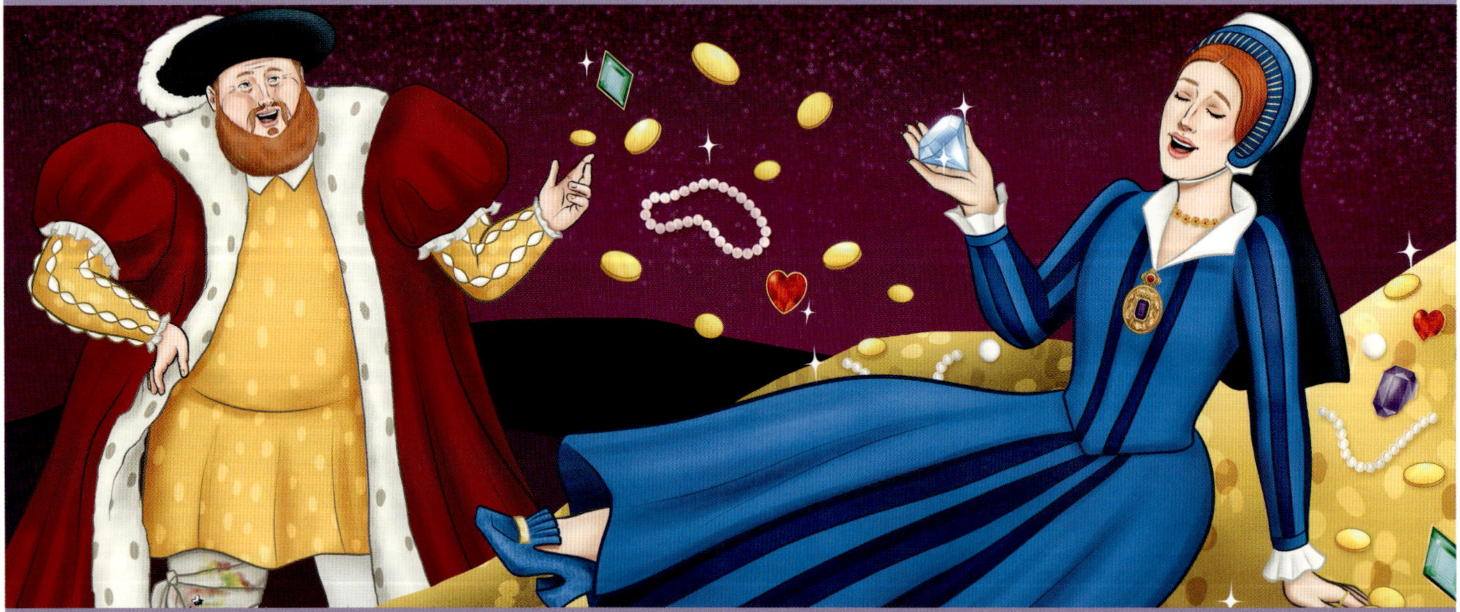

. . . the king was more than *thirty* years older than her, and an old jousting wound on his leg oozed stinky pus. Still, Henry was generous, showering Catherine in pearls and diamonds and so many dresses that she could wear a new one every single day!

Another Tragic Ending

There was much more to Catherine than parties and dresses. She convinced her husband to free several prisoners and when she discovered one woman in the Tower of London didn't have proper clothes, she paid her own tailor to sew a whole new wardrobe for her.

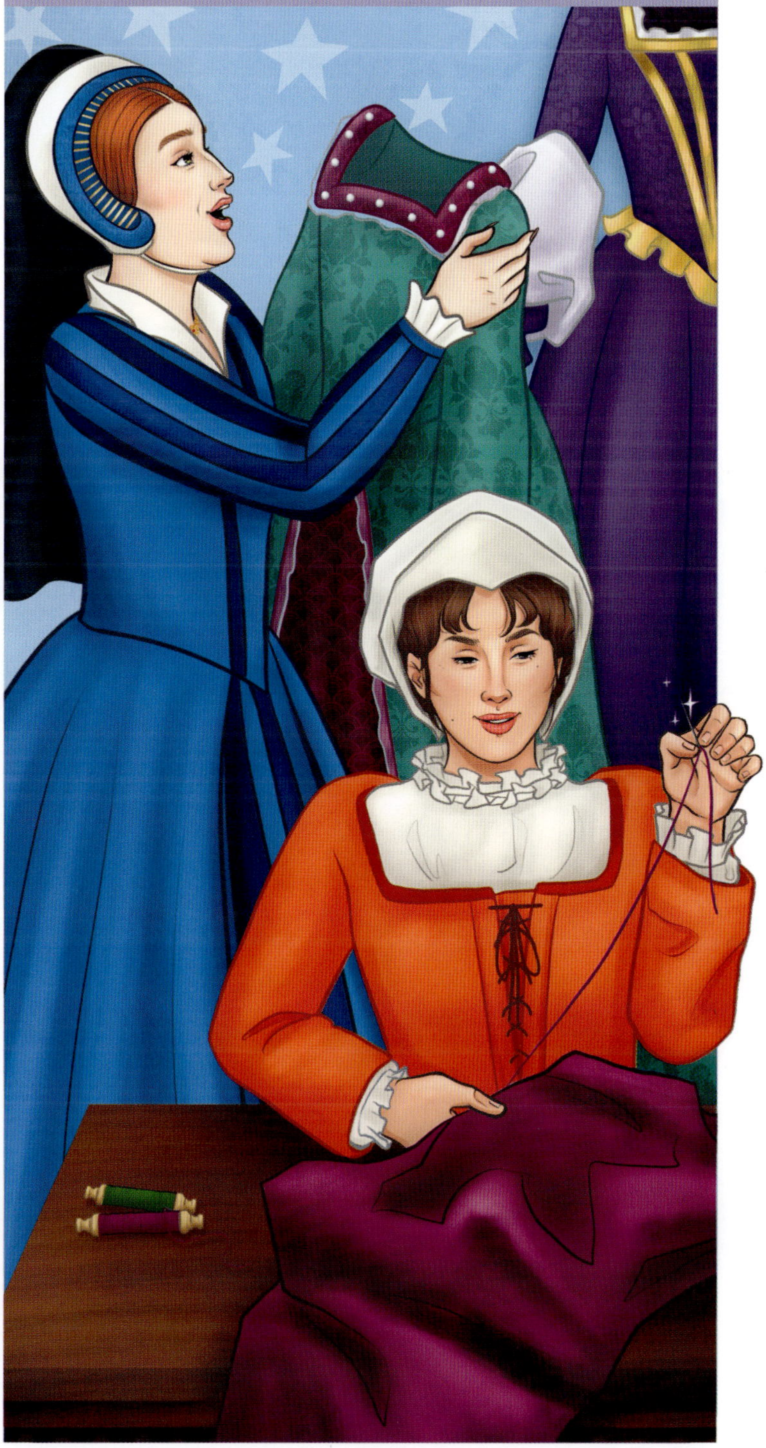

Catherine's reign seemed to be going well . . . until disaster struck when someone snitched to the king about Catherine's former boyfriends. Henry ordered an investigation.

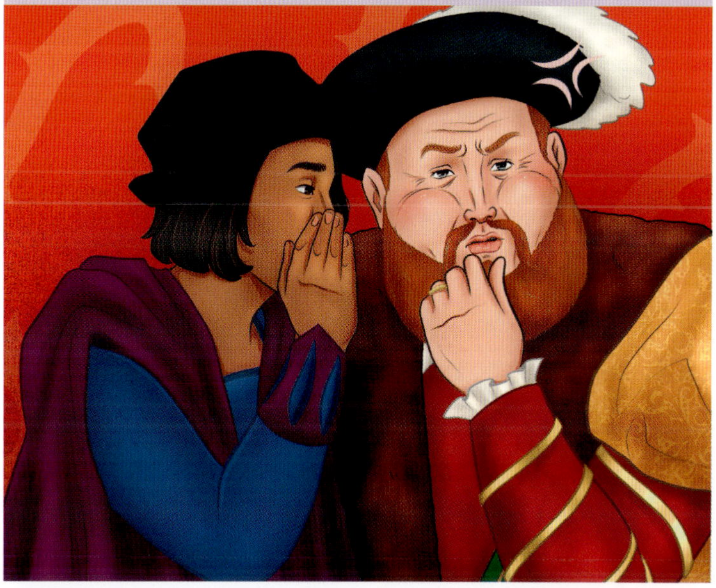

Not only were the rumours true, but Catherine was having a relationship with Thomas Culpepper, one of the king's courtiers. Henry was so outraged that he sent her to the Tower and had her beheaded!

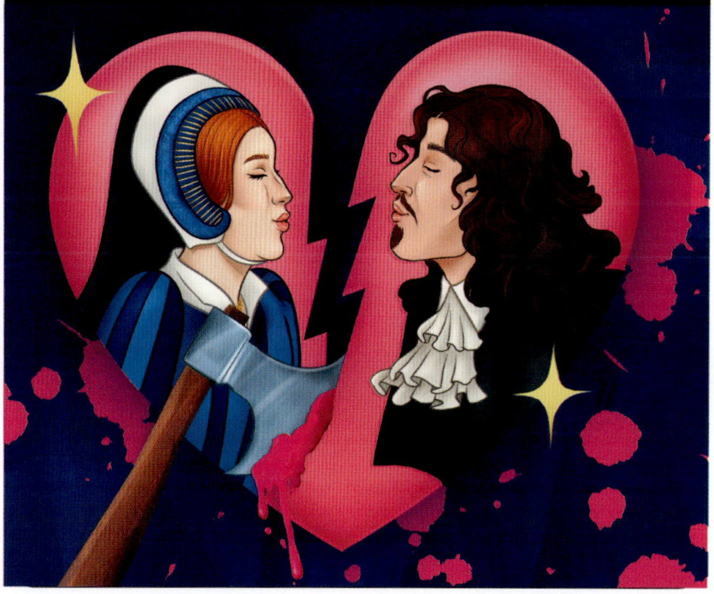

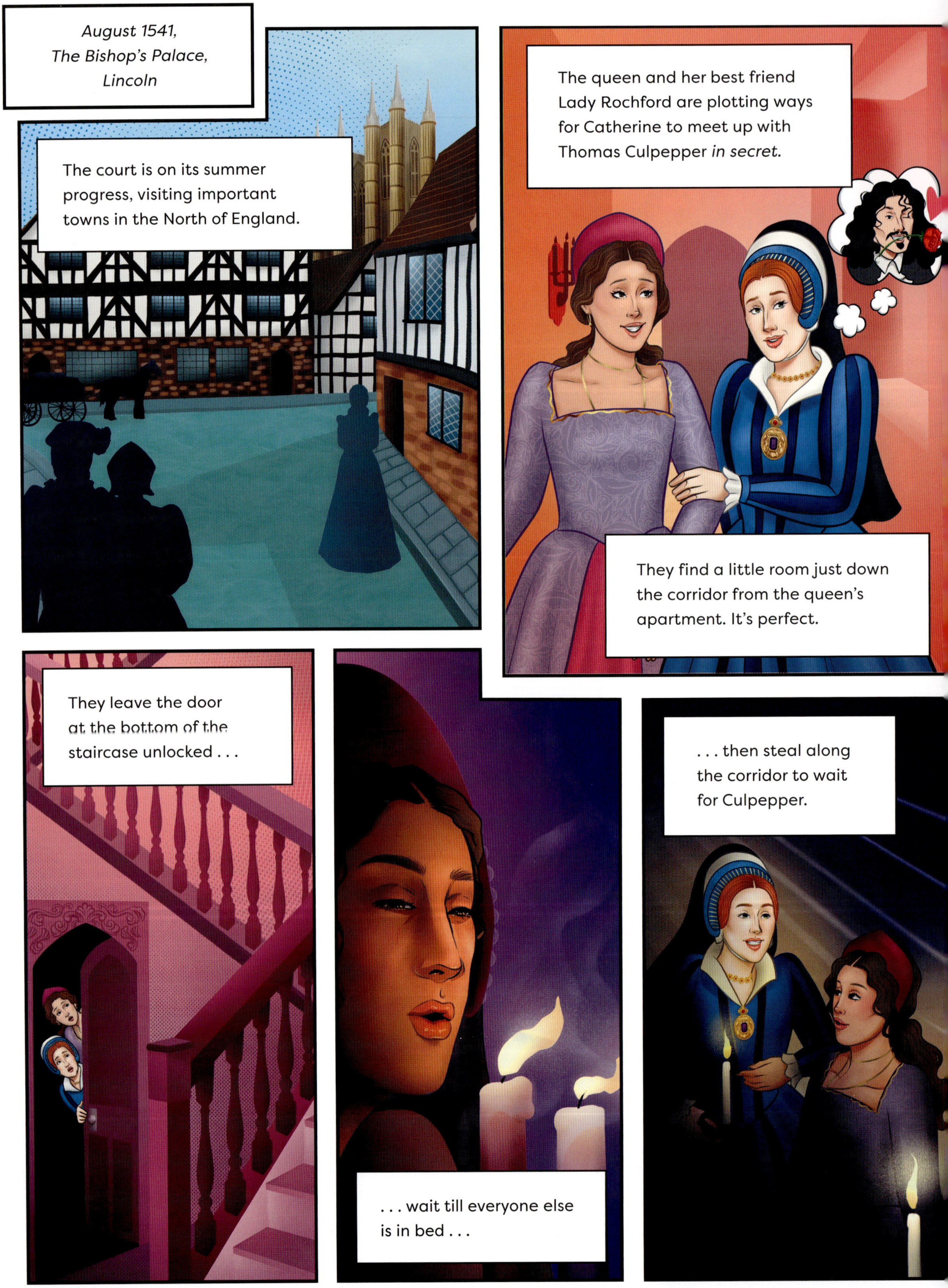

August 1541,
The Bishop's Palace,
Lincoln
The court is on its summer progress, visiting important towns in the North of England.
The queen and her best friend Lady Rochford are plotting ways for Catherine to meet up with Thomas Culpepper *in secret.*
They find a little room just down the corridor from the queen's apartment. It's perfect.
They leave the door at the bottom of the staircase unlocked . . .
. . . wait till everyone else is in bed . . .
. . . then steal along the corridor to wait for Culpepper.

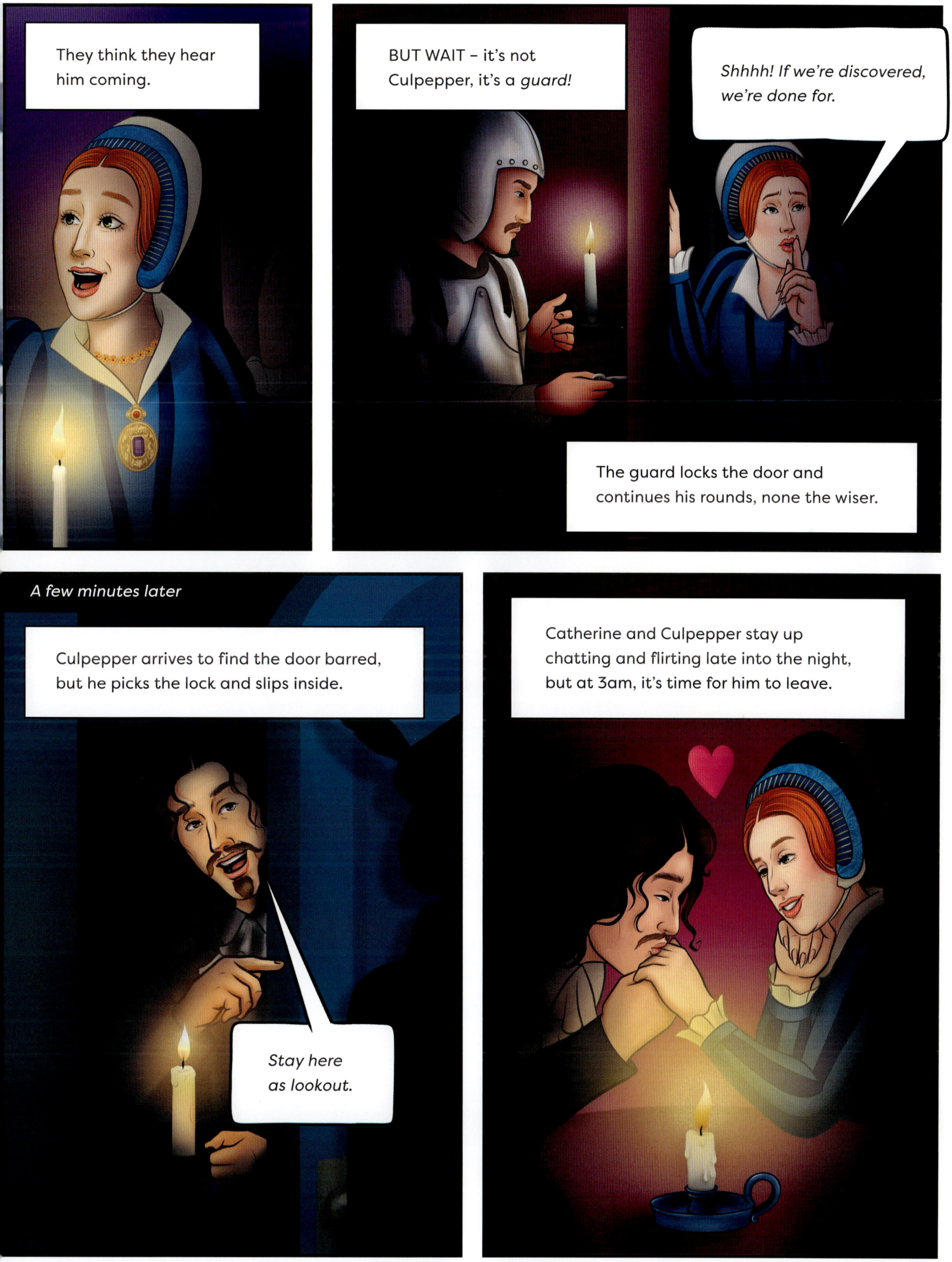
They think they hear him coming.
BUT WAIT – it's not Culpepper, it's a *guard!*
Shhhh! If we're discovered, we're done for.
The guard locks the door and continues his rounds, none the wiser.
A few minutes later
Culpepper arrives to find the door barred, but he picks the lock and slips inside.
Stay here as lookout.
Catherine and Culpepper stay up chatting and flirting late into the night, but at 3am, it's time for him to leave.

KATHERINE PARR

BIOGRAPHY

Katherine's family was wealthy and well-connected at court, but they weren't nobles. Katherine's mother was a lady-in-waiting to Catherine of Aragon, and it's possible that Katherine was actually named after Henry's first queen! Katherine's father died when she was young, but her mother made sure she had the best of educations.

BORN: 1512(ish), either Blackfriars, London or Kendal Castle, Cumbria

EDUCATION: Literature, theology, Latin, French, dancing

MARRIED HENRY VIII: 1543

WIDOWED: 1547

DIED: 1548

OTHER HUSBANDS: Two before Henry, and another one after

CHILDREN: Mary Seymour (by her last husband)

MOTTO: "To Be Useful In All I Do"

Many Marriages

Katherine's first husband, Edward Borough, died just a few years after they married. She soon married again, this time to Lord Latimer of Snape Castle – a powerful Northerner who already had two children and was almost double her age.

Things weren't always easy: when Latimer got caught up in the rebellion known as the Pilgrimage of Grace, Katherine may have been held hostage by the rebels!

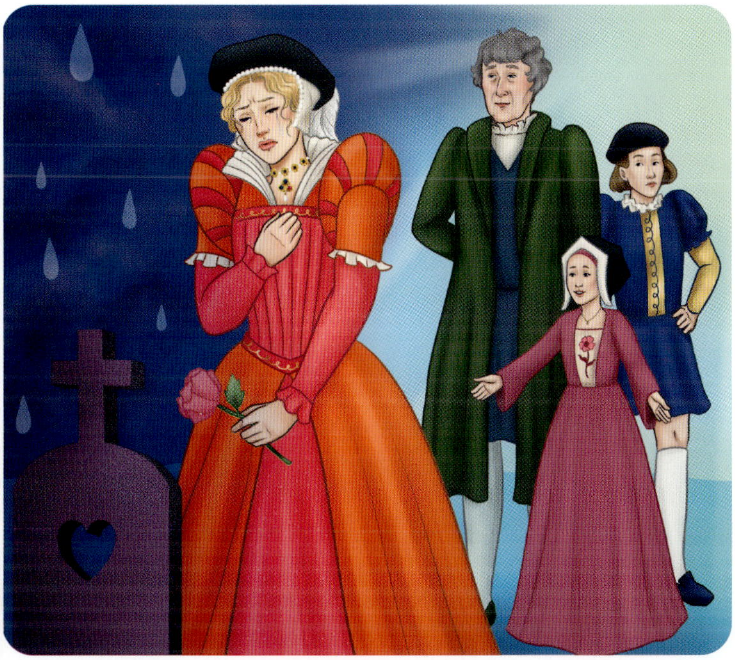

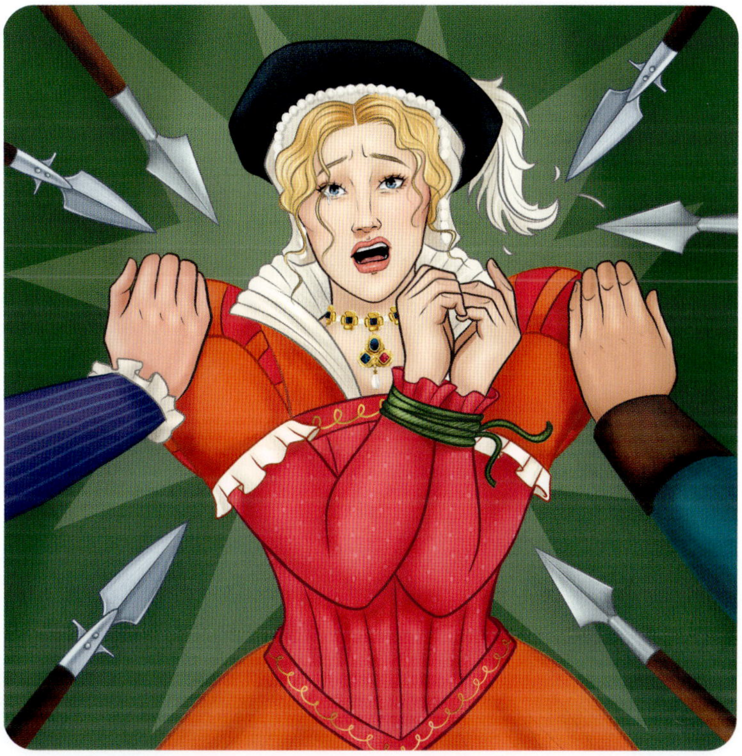

After her second husband died in 1543, Katherine fell in love with Thomas Seymour, brother of Jane Seymour. Katherine hoped to marry him but there was a problem – King Henry had fallen in love with her.

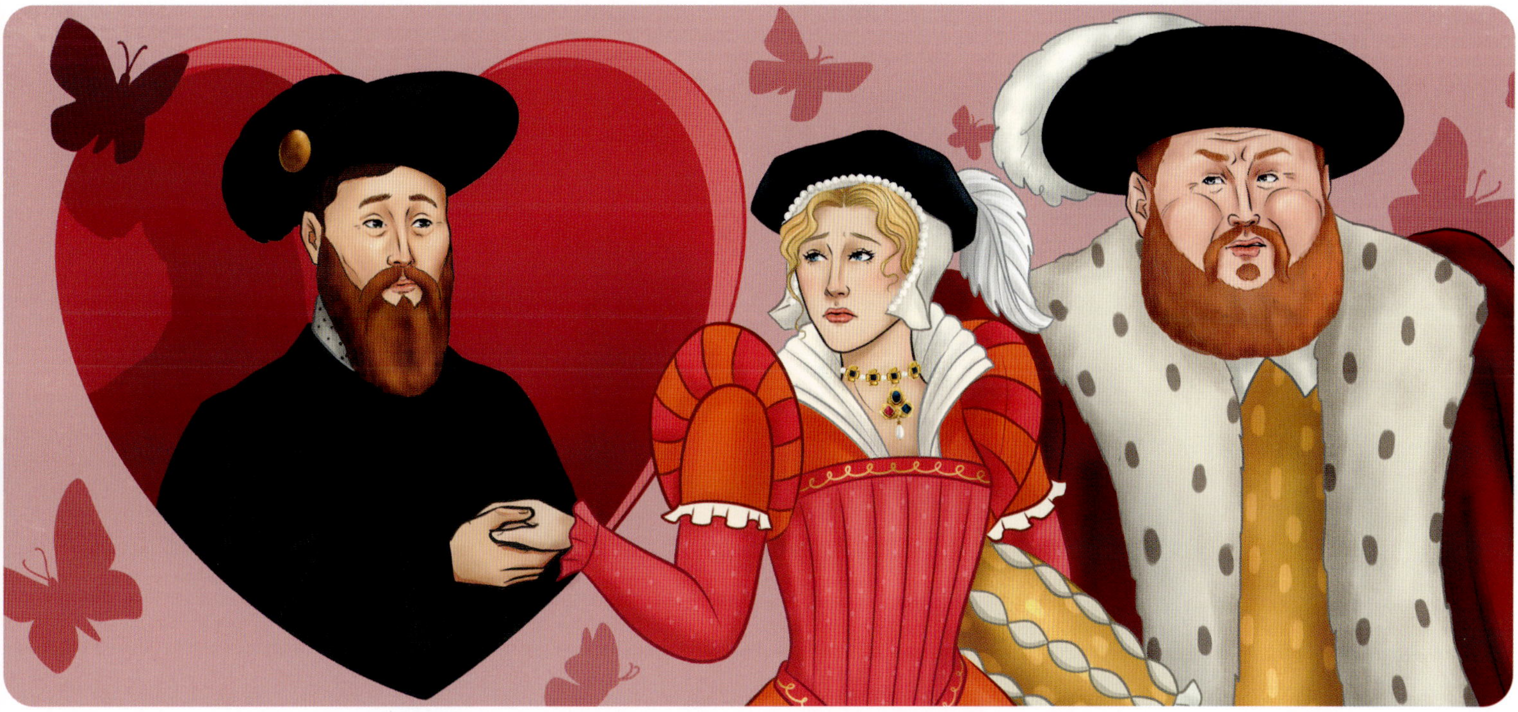

Making the Most of It

When Henry VIII proposed to you, you couldn't really say no – so Katherine and Henry were married in July 1543. Katherine hadn't exactly wanted to be queen, but now she was determined to use her new power to her advantage.

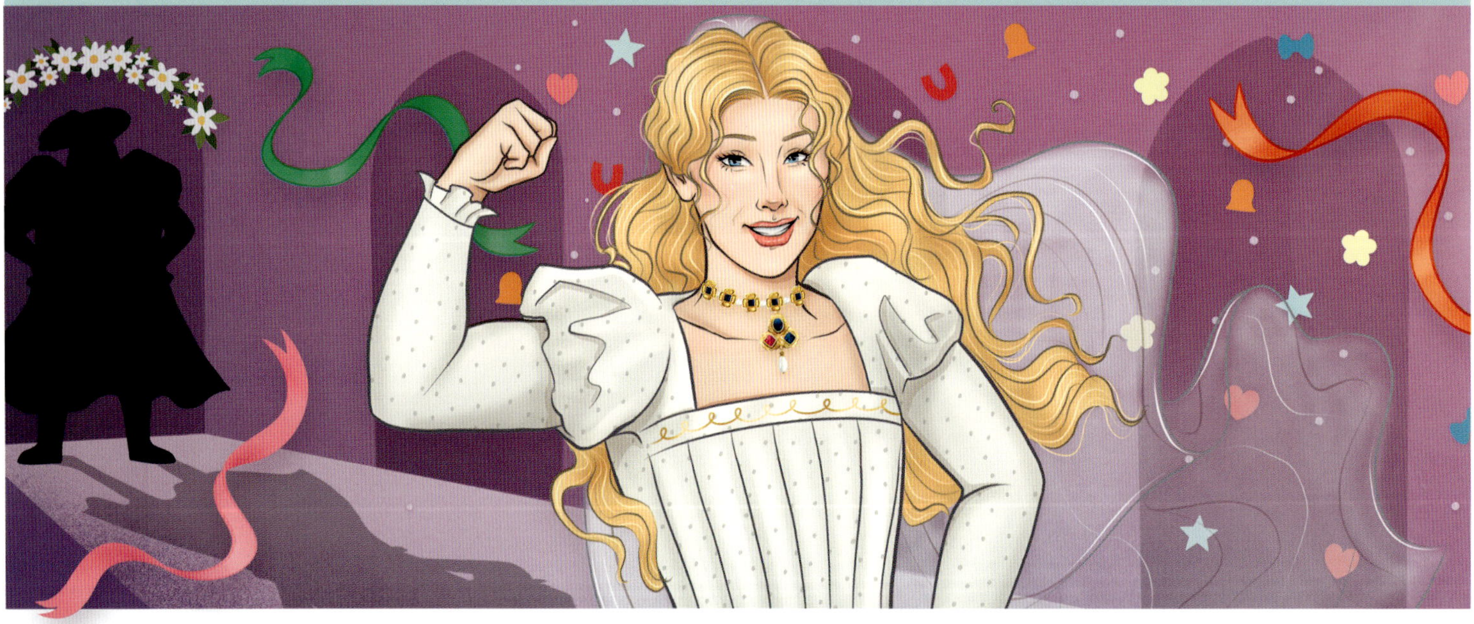

Katherine used her newfound wealth to support artists, writers and musicians. But her real interest was in religion; she read banned books and encouraged Henry to pursue radical protestant religious reforms.

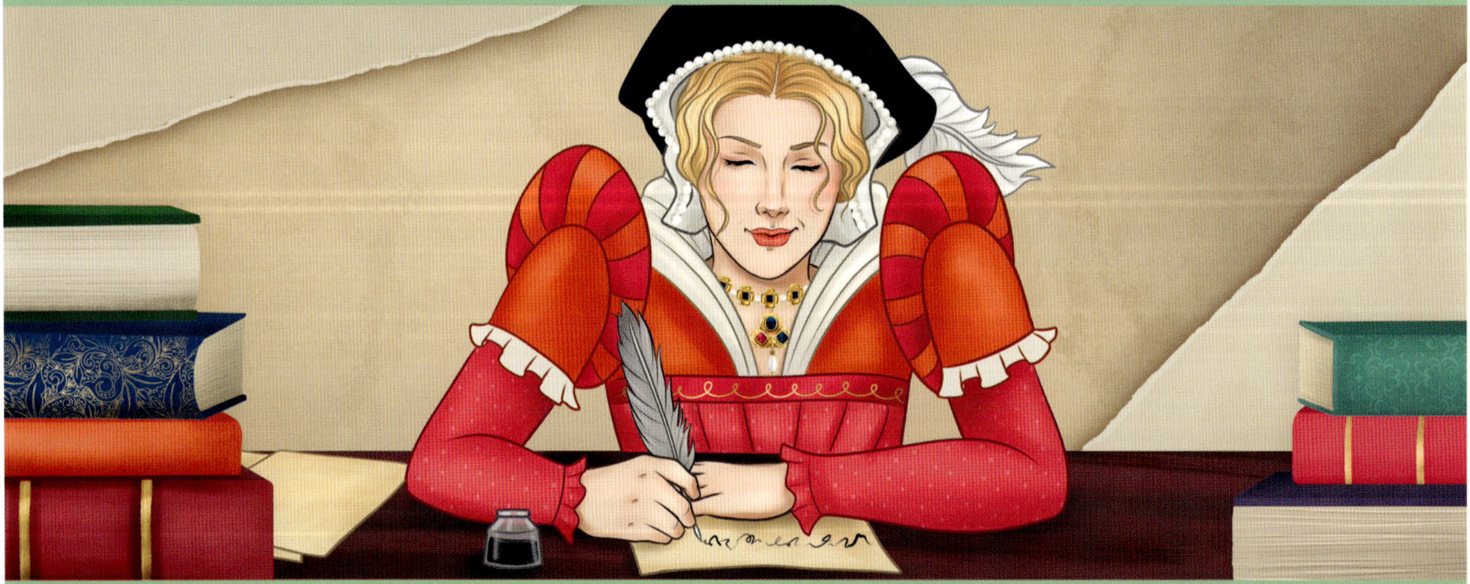

Katherine even wrote books of her own about religion – making her the first EVER woman to publish a book in English under her own name!

Quite the Queen

The queen made sure her family were promoted up the ranks of the aristocracy, but she smoothed things over in Henry's family too. She personally oversaw the education of Princess Elizabeth and Prince Edward.

When Henry went to fight the French in 1544, he trusted Katherine enough to make her his regent. She was in charge and although she had a council of men, every decision had to go through her.

Katherine's intelligence and outspokenness scared some of the powerful men in Henry's court – especially the ones who disagreed with her about religion.

When Henry died in 1547 Katherine inherited a fortune, and the freedom to do whatever she liked with it! Just a few months later she married Thomas Seymour, the man she'd loved before Henry, but sadly died after giving birth to their daughter Mary in 1548.

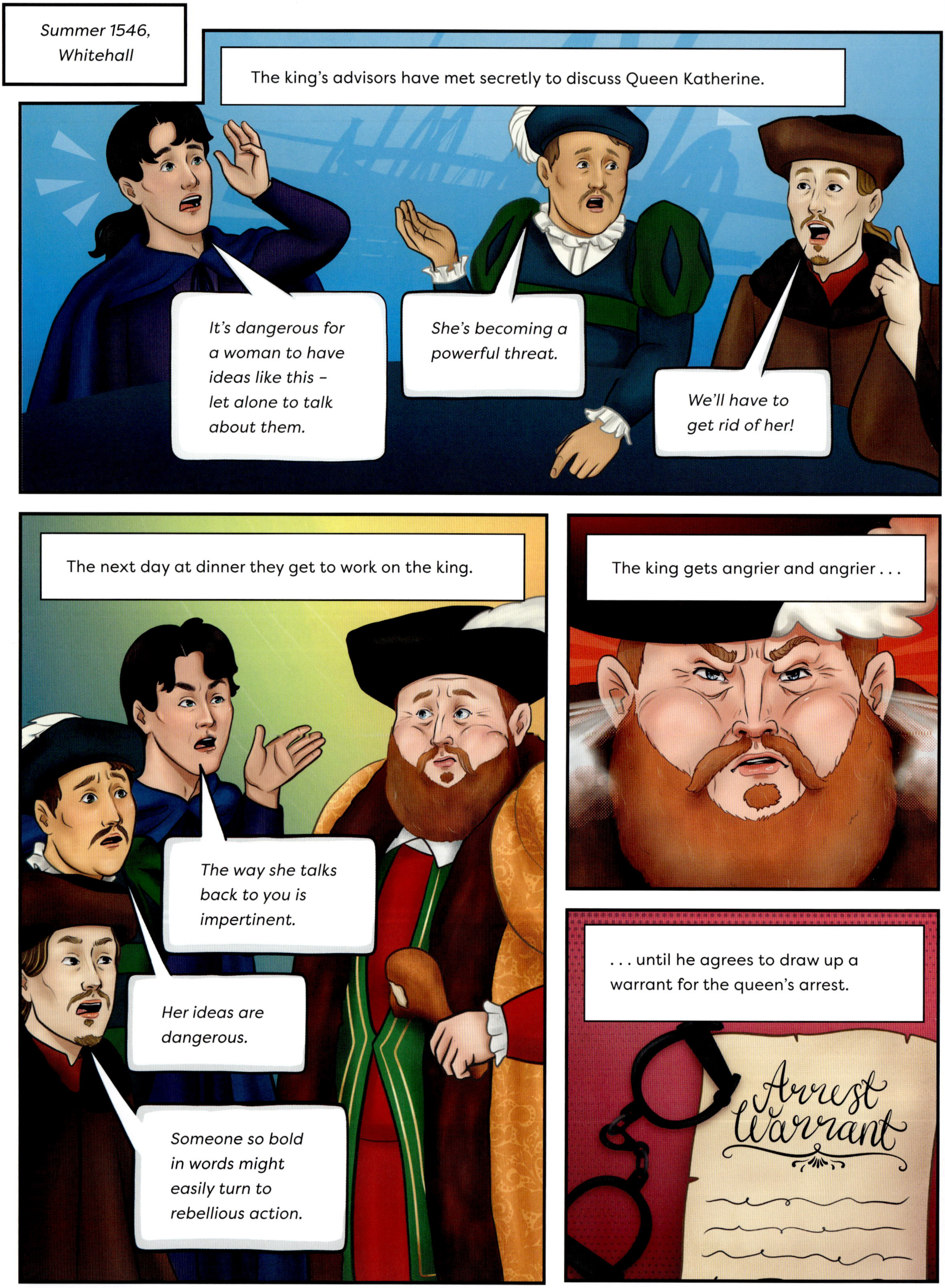
Summer 1546, Whitehall
The king's advisors have met secretly to discuss Queen Katherine.
It's dangerous for a woman to have ideas like this – let alone to talk about them.
She's becoming a powerful threat.
We'll have to get rid of her!
The next day at dinner they get to work on the king.
The way she talks back to you is impertinent.
Her ideas are dangerous.
Someone so bold in words might easily turn to rebellious action.
The king gets angrier and angrier . . .
. . . until he agrees to draw up a warrant for the queen's arrest.
Arrest Warrant

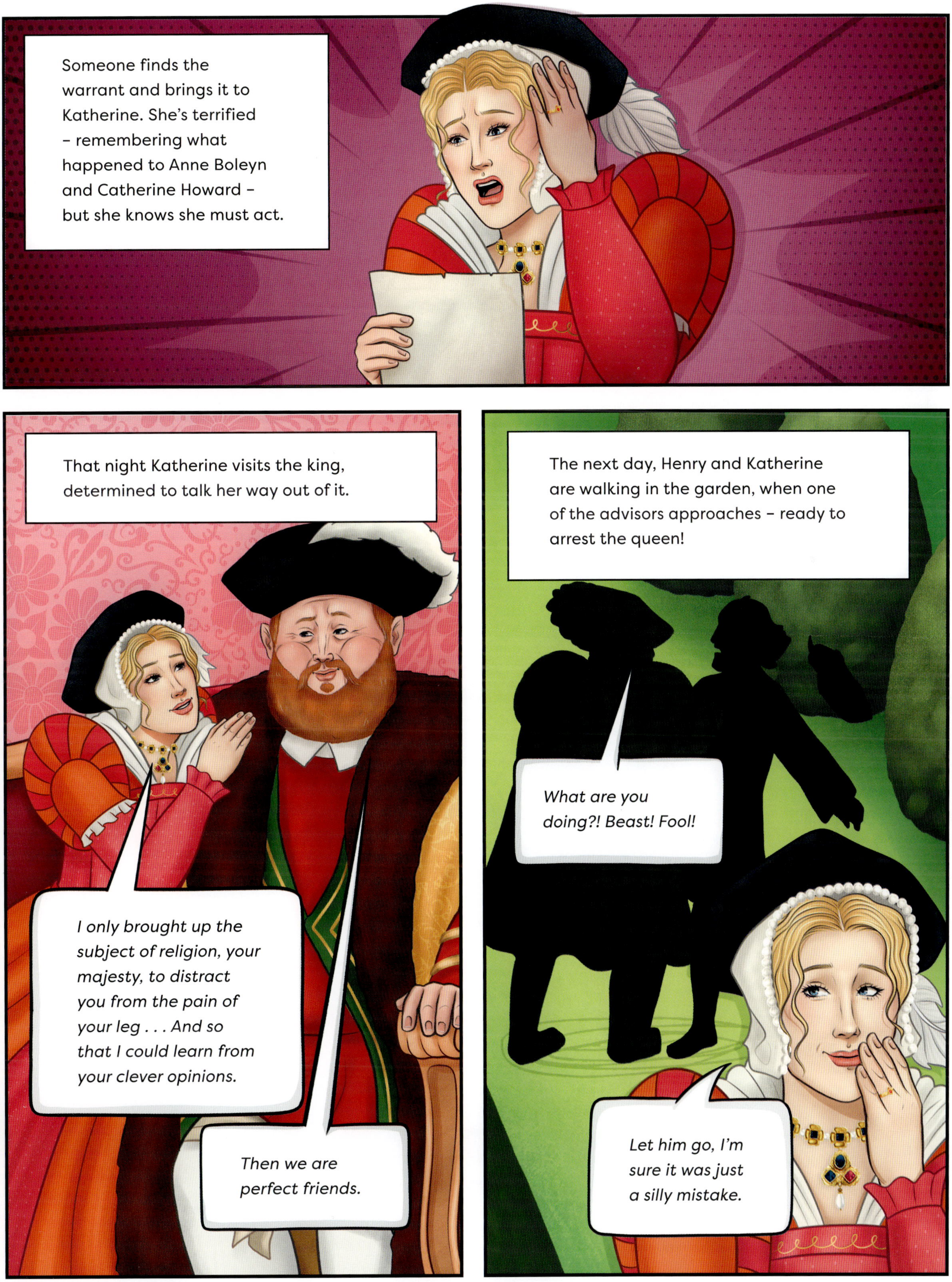
Someone finds the warrant and brings it to Katherine. She's terrified – remembering what happened to Anne Boleyn and Catherine Howard – but she knows she must act.
That night Katherine visits the king, determined to talk her way out of it.
I only brought up the subject of religion, your majesty, to distract you from the pain of your leg . . . And so that I could learn from your clever opinions.
Then we are perfect friends.
The next day, Henry and Katherine are walking in the garden, when one of the advisors approaches – ready to arrest the queen!
What are you doing?! Beast! Fool!
Let him go, I'm sure it was just a silly mistake.

The Tudor Family Tree

Arthur, Prince of Wales
(1486–1502)

As the oldest son, Arthur was heir to the English throne, until he died young.

Henry VII
(1457–1509)

Took the English throne by force at the battle of Bosworth, beginning the Tudor Dynasty.

Henry VIII
(1491–1547)

Confident and dashing in his youth but increasingly tyrannical and paranoid as his reign went on.

Elizabeth of York
(1466–1503)

The niece of King Richard III, who Henry VII had killed at Bosworth, married Henry VII to stabilise his dynasty.

Mary Tudor
(1496–1533)

Henry VIII's sisters, who went on to secure alliances with Scotland and France through marriages.

Margaret Tudor
(1489–1541)

 = Married

M

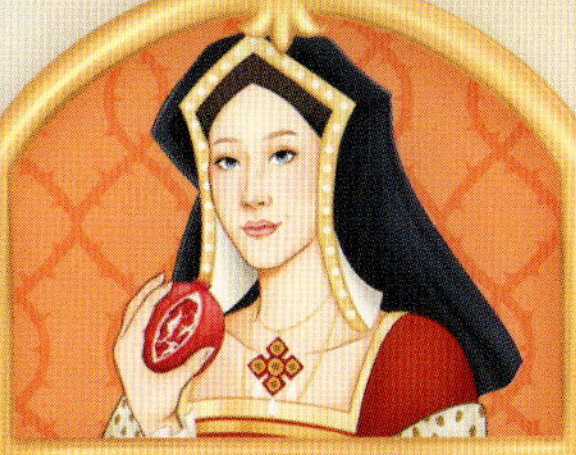

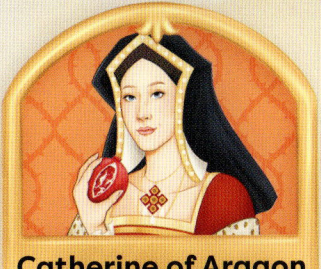

Catherine of Aragon
(1485–1536)

A strong, principled, and stubborn Spanish princess who became an ambassador.

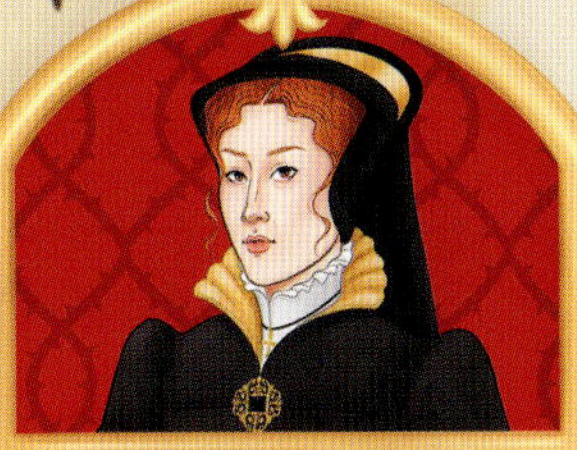

Mary I
(1516–1558)

The first woman to rule England in her own right.

M

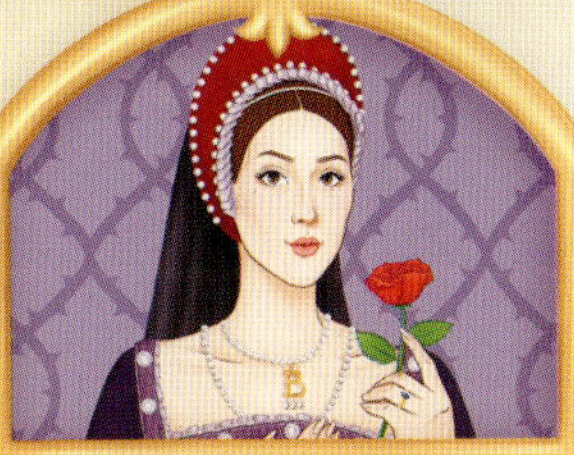

Anne Boleyn
(c. 1501–1536)

Charismatic, ambitious and extremely intelligent.

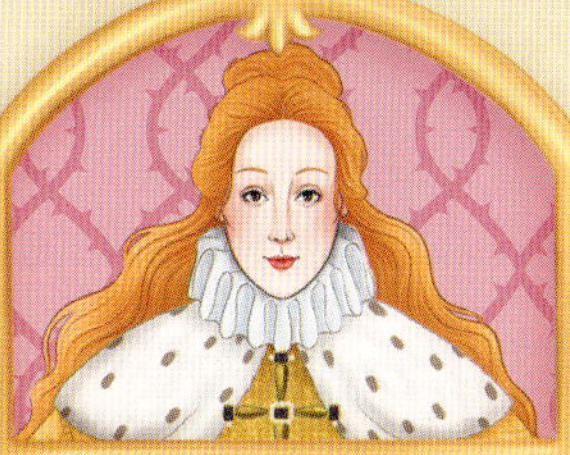

Elizabeth I
(1533–1603)

The last Tudor monarch. Her long and stable reign was celebrated as a golden age.

M

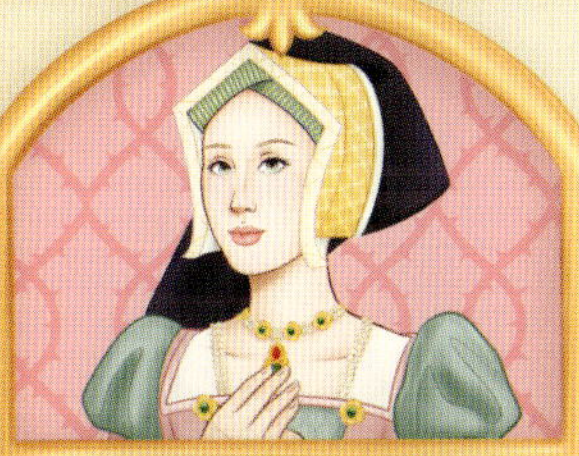

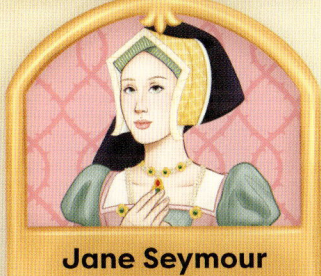

Jane Seymour
(c. 1508–1537)

Played up to the image of the quiet and obedient wife.

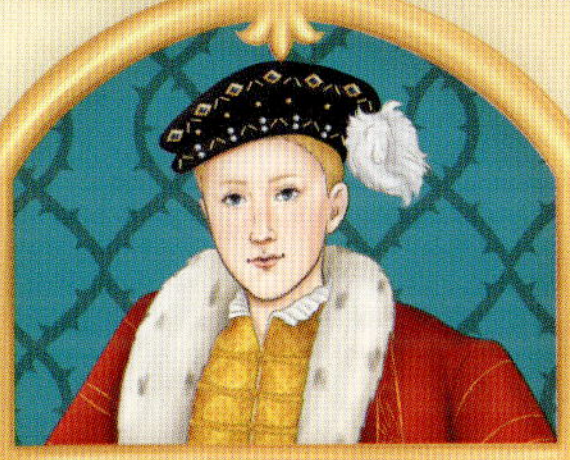

Edward VI
(1537–1553)

Henry's longed-for son, Edward became king at nine years old and died at just fifteen. Because of his youth, political decisions were made by his regents.

M

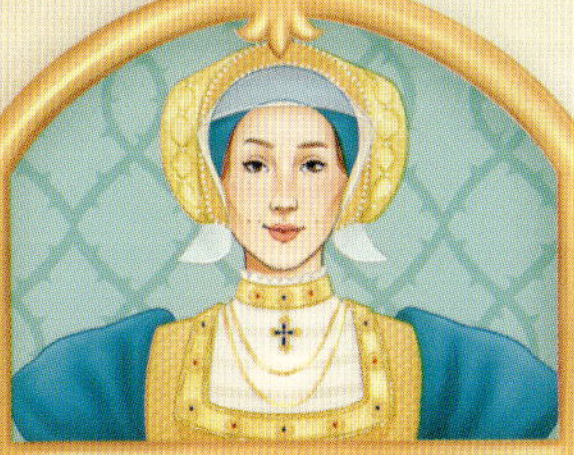

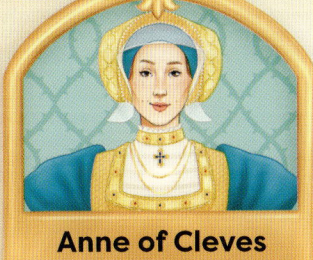

Anne of Cleves
(1515–1557)

Sensibly agreed to Henry's request for a divorce, gaining status and independence.

M

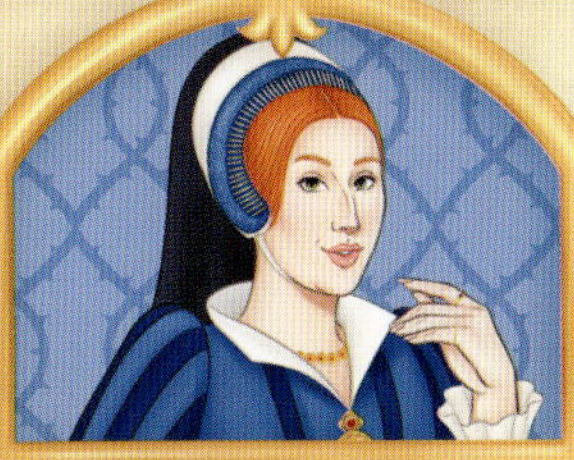

Catherine Howard
(c. 1522–1542)

Very young, beautiful and fun-loving.

M

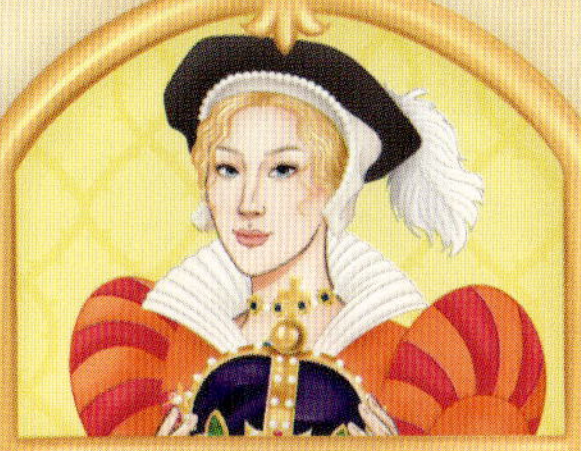

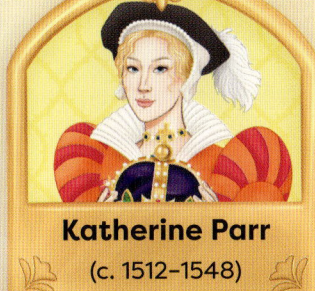

Katherine Parr
(c. 1512–1548)

Clever, rational and experienced.

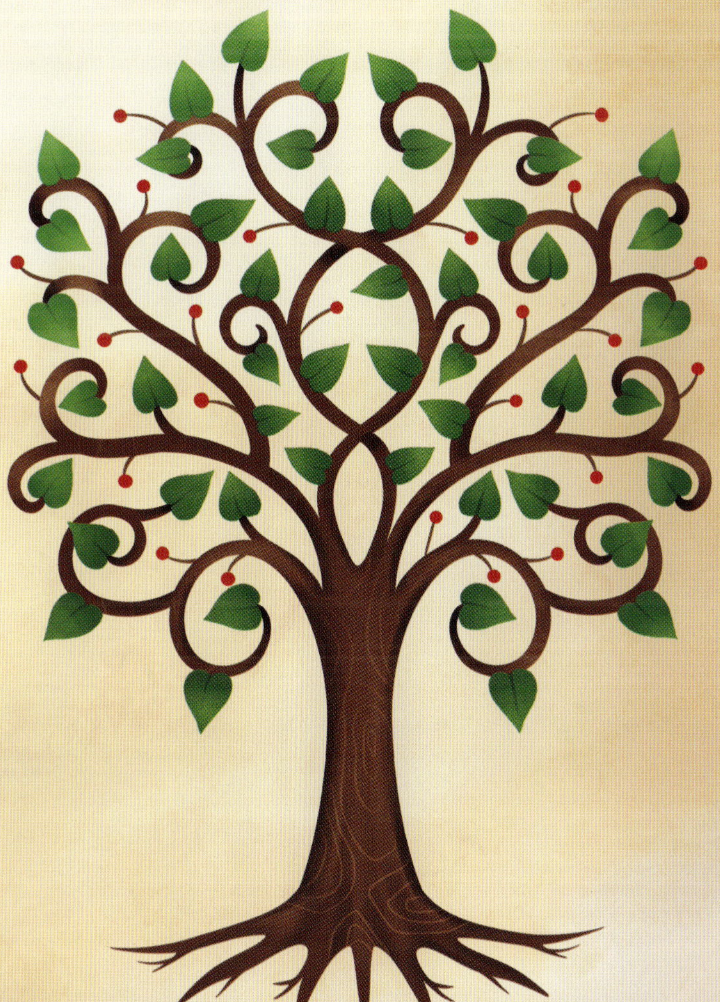

Tudor Family Timeline

1485 – Henry VII is crowned king, and the Tudor era begins.

1491 – Henry VIII is born.

1501 – Catherine of Aragon marries Henry's older brother Arthur, but he soon dies.

1509 – Henry VII dies, Henry VIII becomes king and marries Catherine of Aragon.

1513 – Under the regency of Catherine of Aragon, the English army defeats the Scottish king at the Battle of Flodden.

1516 – Catherine of Aragon gives birth to a daughter, Mary.

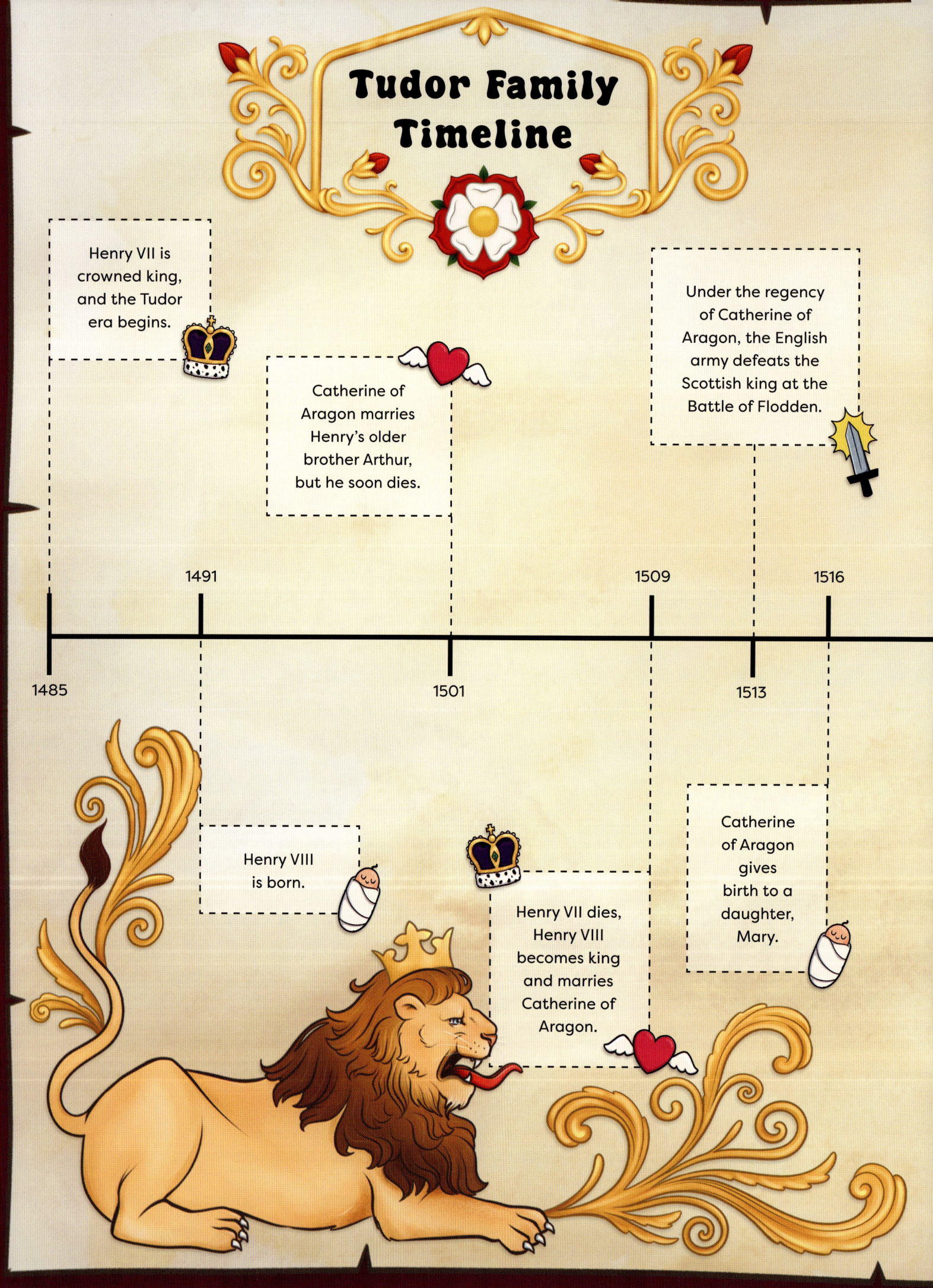

- **1527** – Henry asks the Pope to annul his marriage to Catherine of Aragon.
- **1533** – Henry marries Anne Boleyn and divorces Catherine of Aragon.
- **1533** – Anne gives birth to a daughter, Elizabeth.
- **1534** – Henry is declared head of the new Church of England.
- **1536** – Catherine of Aragon dies.
- **1536** – Anne Boleyn is beheaded and Henry marries Jane Seymour.
- **1537** – Jane Seymour dies after giving birth to a son, Edward.
- **1540** – Henry marries Anne of Cleves, but soon divorces her and marries Catherine Howard.
- **1542** – Catherine Howard is beheaded.
- **1543** – Henry marries Katherine Parr.
- **1545** – Katherine publishes her first book and Henry makes her his regent.
- **1547** – Henry dies and Edward VI becomes king.
- **1548** – Katherine Parr dies in childbirth.
- **1553** – Edward VI dies and Mary I becomes queen.
- **1557** – Anne of Cleves dies.
- **1558** – Mary I dies and Elizabeth I becomes queen.

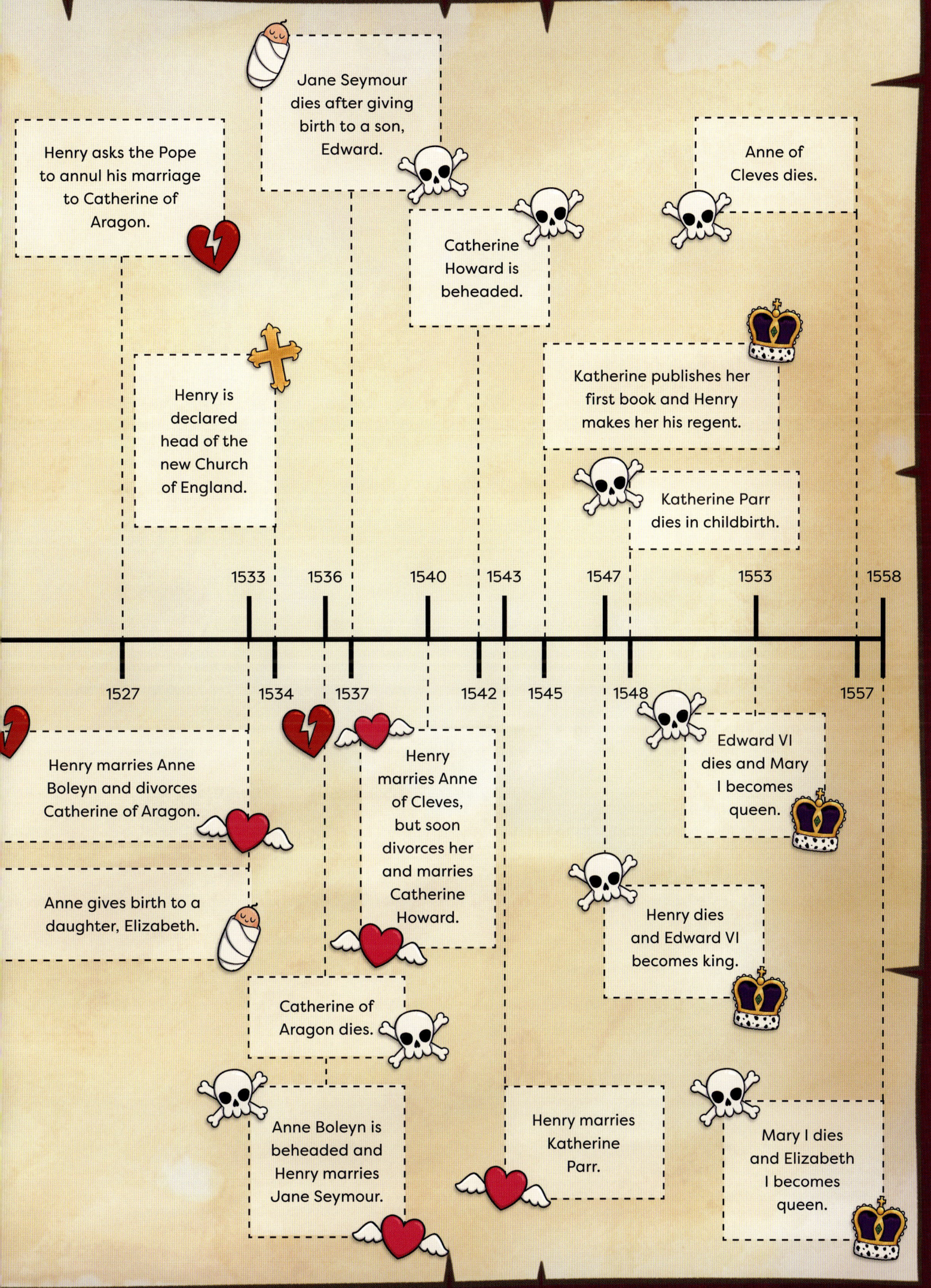

Henry VIII's Children

Edward VI

Edward was only nine years old when he became king and he spent most of his coronation giggling at a tightrope walker! Although Edward's political decisions were guided by a council of regents because of his age, he had strong ideas of his own. His reign saw radical anti-Catholic religious reforms, but Edward also found time to set up a number of free grammar schools.

MOTHER: Jane Seymour
BORN: 1537
REIGNED: 1547–1553
MARRIED: Bit young for that
MOTTO: "God and My Right"

Mary I

Mary was torn between her warring parents after they divorced, but despite huge pressure she refused to give up the Catholic faith she'd inherited from her mother. After Edward died, Mary raised an army and fought for her throne against those who wanted a Protestant ruler. She won and became the first woman ever to rule England in her own right.

As queen, Mary tried to make England Catholic again. She got her "Bloody" nickname for burning Protestants at the stake, but all the other Tudor monarchs executed people too; if history is written by the winners, Mary's bad reputation might be as much the result of her gender and religion as her actions.

MOTHER: Catherine of Aragon
BORN: 1516
REIGNED: 1553–1558
MARRIED: Yes, to Philip II of Spain, meaning Mary was Queen of Spain as well as England
NICKNAME: "Bloody Mary"
MOTTO: "Truth is the Daughter of Time"

Elizabeth I

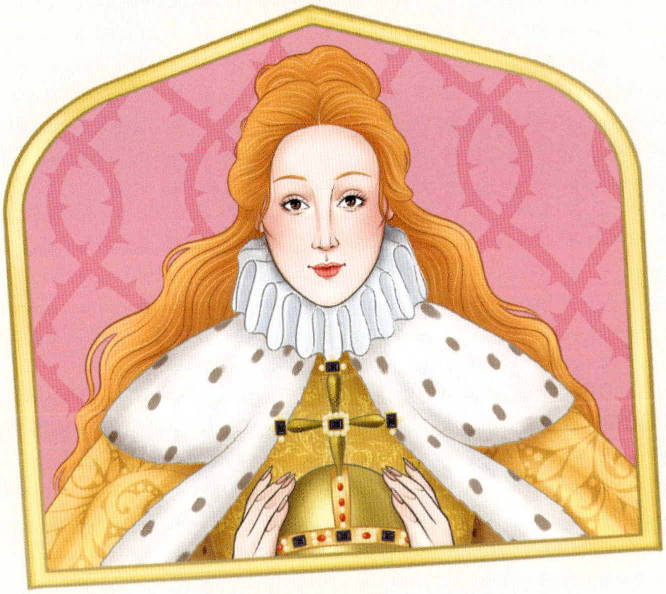

MOTHER: Anne Boleyn

BORN: 1533

REIGNED: 1558–1603

MARRIED: Never!

NICKNAME: “Gloriana”

MOTTO: “Always the Same”

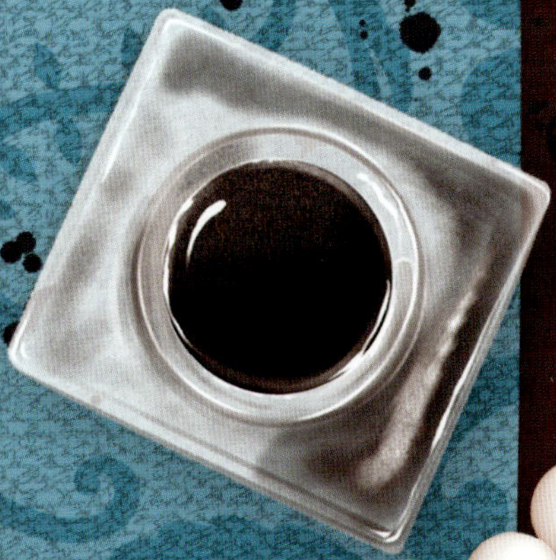

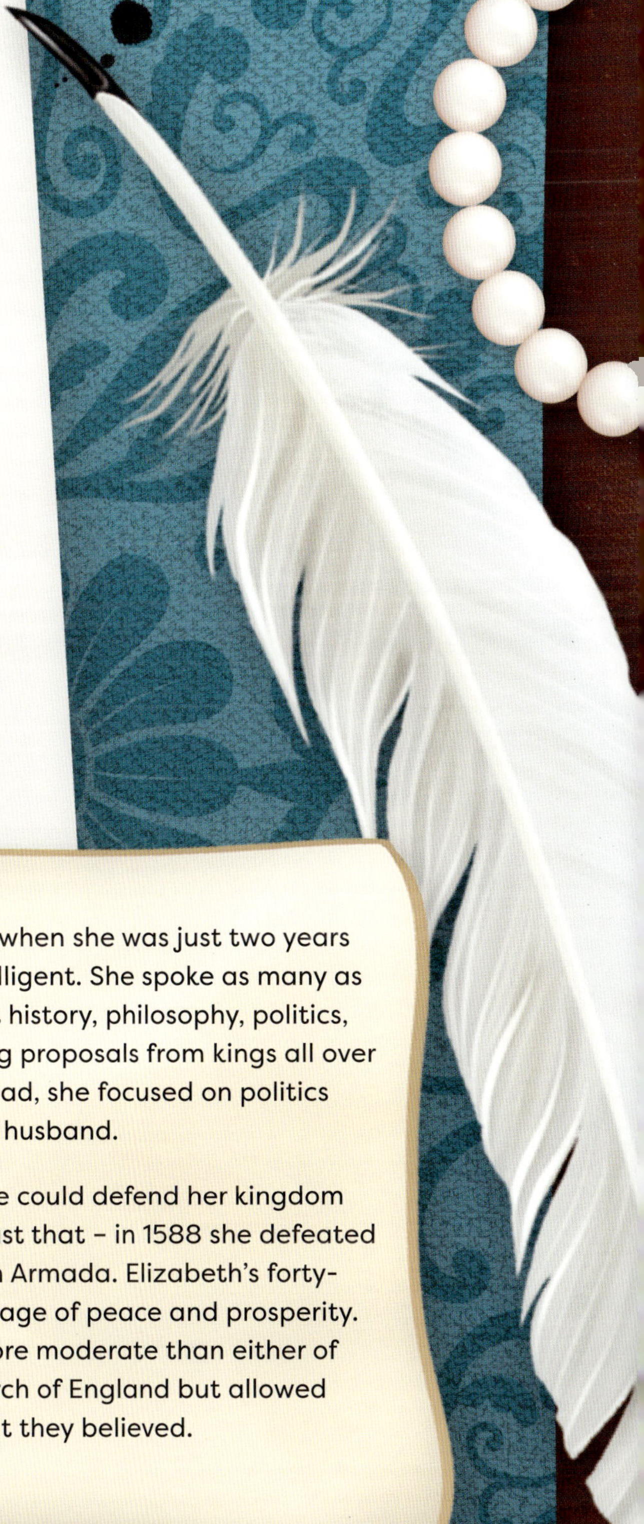

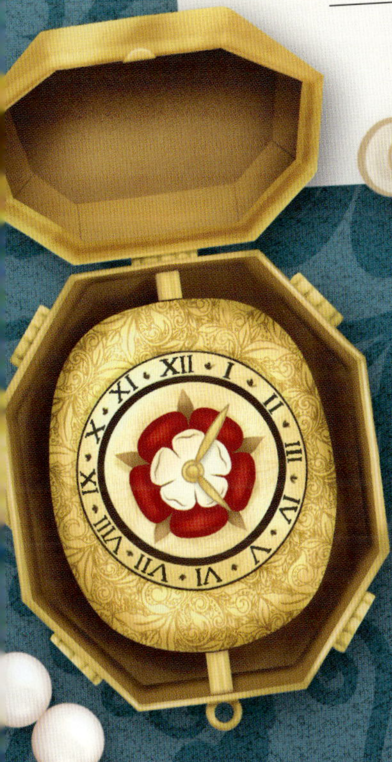

Like her mother, who was beheaded when she was just two years old, Elizabeth was exceptionally intelligent. She spoke as many as nine languages and knew a lot about history, philosophy, politics, religion and rhetoric. Despite receiving proposals from kings all over Europe, Elizabeth never married; instead, she focused on politics and refused to share her power with a husband.

Elizabeth was determined to prove she could defend her kingdom just as well as any man, and she did just that – in 1588 she defeated a huge invasion known as the Spanish Armada. Elizabeth’s forty-five-year reign was seen as a golden age of peace and prosperity. Elizabeth’s religious policies were more moderate than either of her siblings: she reinstated the Church of England but allowed people a degree of freedom in what they believed.